JACK M. COHEN

The Freedom Frameworks

*Infinite Possibilities to Achieve Career Independence
On Your Own Terms*

Contact Information for Darkknight Ventures, LLC

1260 Snowbunny Lane

Aspen, Colorado 81611

(312) 543-5872

Email: Jcohen@darkknightventures.net

Sign up for Jack's updates at www.darkknightventures.net.

The life journeys I have always treasured the most were those of my wife and children.

All I ever wanted in life was to be their sidekick and not let them down. I learned, and I experienced; all I wanted was to be able to share my learnings to support them in the optimization of their personal journeys.

This book is dedicated to Nancy, Lindsay, Jared, Alec, Wyatt, Brandon, Rachel, and Niki. With love, respect, deep affection and admiration.

Definition of iconoclast:

a person who challenges beliefs and
practices that are widely accepted.

The World According to Jack

Contents

Foreword

My first memory of the author, Jack Cohen, dates back more than four decades when we were both students at Stanford University. Even then, Jack demonstrated a propensity for offering career advice when he suggested I leverage my experience as a reporter for the *Stanford Daily* to one day launching my own company. He even came up with the name: I Write. In fact, I did write, for several years, as a business reporter. And true to the subtitle of this book, over the past four-plus decades since matriculating from our shared alma mater, I have pursued what has felt like "infinite possibilities" over the course of my career, with Jack continuing to play a significant influence as a dear friend, client, and champion.

Today I wear two hats: as an academic teaching at a top ten US university and as the principal of my own consulting firm offering a range of leadership and organizational development services. Both roles have required me to pour through hundreds of academic studies on leadership and professional development as well as be current on the plethora of popular books with titles touting the next miracle drug for career success.

Being more than conversant with this field, I can safely state *The Freedom Frameworks* joins a very crowded party with an impressive guest list of thought leaders. You need only to walk through any airport terminal to spot dozens of kiosks with the latest *New York Times* best sellers promoting get-ahead strategies to climb the proverbial corporate ladder. From Spencer Johnson's classic *Who Moved My Cheese?* to Marshall Goldsmith's best seller *What Got You Here Won't Get You There,* there is no shortage of career self-help books.

Thankfully, *The Freedom Frameworks* breathes new life into this genre and makes its own unique contribution. Jack is the first to admit/point out his frameworks come from his own experiences and professional sweat equity. The "empirical evidence" stems from forty-three years of his impressive career as a maverick in commercial real estate finance, supplemented by his role as a father and husband. The lessons he imparts were hard won.

While the book title is paid off through charming self-effacing stories, rich metaphors, practical tips, and reflection to wrap up each chapter, the subtitle hints at the most potent message: achieving career independence on your own terms. Imagine the infinite possibilities.

Throughout the book, Jack puts sharp teeth into what has become a hackneyed term. How often are graduate students and young professionals told they have infinite possibilities, only to experience setbacks, failures, and disappointments without a playbook to respond. Jack provocatively points to our "demons" as forces that demand our reckoning.

Each chapter explores an aspect of achieving freedom within the context of professional fulfillment. The structure facilitates insight, learning, and action. In particular, the device used to wrap up each section—Quick Takes and Bringing It All Together—serves as a breadcrumb of sorts for the reader.

A few that hit home for me include the counsel to focus less on outcomes and pay closer attention to the source activities that will lead to the outcomes. His related idea that the pull energy from our future vision is more potent than the push energy we impose on ourselves to reach our goals. Another fan favorite (I am clearly a fan!) is the simple wisdom of being reliable. Consistently having someone's back (and front) is a character trait that serves us well, regardless of our age and stage.

Throughout this enjoyable and entertaining quick read, Jack pays homage to his own superhero: Batman. As the founder of Darkknight Ventures, Jack has taken the storied legend of Batman to heart. He brings us into his bat cave and invites us to examine the state of our own Gotham City. In addition to Batman, Tarzan, Curious George, and other characters make an appearance to underscore the point of the chapter.

What really distinguishes this book from so many others in the genre is the vulnerability exuded and anecdotes shared by the author. While there are ample examples from Jack's vast experience in commercial real estate, some of the most poignant and powerful lessons learned came through interactions with his children. I found myself internalizing many of the ideas, insights, and tips through the lens of a parent as much as I did as a professional.

In his note, Jack says of the book: *If it accelerates your success or helps you through a rough patch, I'm pleased.* There is no doubt in my mind that both sides of that equation will prove out. Personally, I can attest to the fact that my slope of growth has been accelerated by Freedom Frameworks. You'll have to read until at least chapter 9 to fully appreciate the reference.

Dr. Aleen Bayard, CEO/Founder of Transformative Consulting (aleenbayard.com)

Preface

A Note from Jack

I have always loved superheroes—none more so than Batman. Unlike all the others with super strength, X-ray vision, or other supernatural abilities, Batman didn't have any superpowers. He was just a man, albeit an iconoclast, with a mission.

Bruce Wayne was inspired to serve and protect the people of Gotham through an alter ego. He created a new vision from his current reality to his intended future with a transition plan that included going rogue. Blessed with intellectual and economic resources, he leveraged those resources to invent new technologies and equip himself with tools that, when affixed to his utility belt, offered him an edge. Over time, he optimized his greatest asset, himself, becoming an expert deploying his tools and leveraging himself into excellence to fulfill his vision of helping others in need of support.

Batman believed in the good of humanity and wanted to help the citizens of Gotham optimize their journey and be free to get home safely in the dark of night. This Dark Knight metaphor has served as the ideal metaphor for my mentor capital and consulting business, my private holding company, Darkknight Ventures LLC (www.DarkknightVentures.net).

I believe it's okay, perhaps even required, to have an iconoclastic, even rogue, mindset (not being an effect of societal and corporate norms) that is true to your belief system and that allows you to think and act differently from the conventional norm in order to achieve *your* dreams. This nonconformist position and thought process is less about what others think and more about what you would like to accomplish no matter what others think, believe, know, and do.

Like Batman, I too, desire and excel when I'm experiencing personal freedom. I believe that freedom is a mindset that everyone can cultivate and embody. I am talking about the kind of freedom that allows an individual to pursue their dreams. This book is a collection of frameworks that answer how people can start from the context of freedom and tactically optimize their journey. Any journey. My hope with this book is to supply you with some tools to equip yourself in your individual mission.

I have spent more than forty-three years as a business professional, entrepreneur, manager (hired from outside a firm's ecosystem), consultant, investor, and operator, primarily in the commercial real estate finance industry. During that time, and as a lifetime learner who has acquired many skills, experiences, and relationships—good, bad, memorable, and forgettable ones—I have collected a useful set of tools consisting of frameworks, sound bites, stories, and experiences that are holstered in my utility belt.

My mission with this book is to share many of those tools. Each tool will optimize the most valuable asset you have—you—and collectively, become your Freedom Frameworks.

While I hope you don't find it cheesy, I could not resist using the Dark Knight metaphor as a backdrop to explain some of these tools and mindsets.

However, Batman's ideas and ideals were not enough. Innovative tools created and applied appropriately were required to accelerate Bruce Wayne and Batman's success. These tools added leverage for his efforts, which delivered more effective power than he could have mustered through his own willpower. So, too, for us mere mortals.

I come from a place of having learned and experienced so that I may teach others, in hopes of helping you experience more of the freedom you seek in your life. In this book's context, I'm referring to career independence. Still, whether professionally, personally, individually, or for the familial, we could all use a strategic advantage—or edge—to help us evolve to epic levels. And that is what this book is about.

Life isn't linear. As John Lennon once said, "Life is what happens when you are busy making other plans." My dad used to say, "Man plans; God laughs." Louis Pasteur once said that "chance favors the prepared mind." Although we can prepare ourselves to achieve an optimal outcome, rarely can we anticipate what we will need to become in the future. We need to be fluid with our skill sets, possess unconscious competence everywhere we can, and be ready for the unexpected challenge. With this in mind, I've outlined various tools that are more generically applied than specifically and, therefore, will need to be available for use broadly.

As you consider reading on, I confess that I have zero expectation that every reader will pick up and use every framework. In fact, not every framework will speak to, or resonate with, every reader. Please feel free to be a selective learner here. I offer you a curated collection of frameworks that I have developed or acquired along my journey that work for me. My journey is unique to me. As your journey is unique to you. But I believe these frameworks are universal. Therefore, my hope is that you find and embrace the framework(s) that help you effectively optimize your journey.

I did attempt to organize the book the way I would use the frameworks as a practitioner. You, as a learner, can do whatever works best for you. To help accelerate the process, at the end of each chapter, I offer my "Quick Takes" (as in take-home value) and final thoughts attempting to bring it all together for you.

Although I've shared a few stories and details from my life, this book is not intended to flatter me. Rather, if consultants offer answers, and coaches offer questions, as a mentor I see myself as having had decades worth of seemingly interesting and varied experiences that could be valuable and relevant for a young and old professional to learn from. Consider my sharing as a scouting report about life's tendencies and how to prepare for them.

If a sound bite resonates with you, if a framework becomes a tool you can put to work, if a story causes you to laugh or merely relate, then I have accomplished the outcome that I desired. I tried to write a book that's not about "shoulding," as in "you should do this or that." Instead, I want to help you make decisions for yourself. I'm going to share lessons I've learned and advice I've been given to share with you. Feel free to adapt or ignore any you wish.

These Freedom Frameworks come from hardened lessons born from life experiences in a changing world while I was evolving from a young professional to where I am today. You will notice that my laboratory, or bat cave, has been the commercial real estate capital markets. I fervently hope that you will agree that it doesn't really matter what industry you're in or where I learned the hard lessons. As a self-proclaimed iconoclast, I'm confident any, or all, of these universal frameworks have the potential to add significant value to your career journey.

My dream is that at one moment in your future, maybe when you least expect it, a situation on your path presents itself when you (much like Batman) can reach into your utility belt or toolbox and find something that gives you the edge you need at that moment to bypass the challenge and reach your desired outcome. If it accelerates your success or helps you through a rough patch, I am pleased. That's where we're heading.

Jack M. Cohen, June 2024

I

Envision Your Path to Independence

1

Dreams vs. Demons

I'm all out of dreams, I thought to myself.

Despite a relatively prosperous career in commercial real estate finance, at the relatively young age of sixty-six and armed with a strident belief that I'd be vibrant and working well into my nineties, I felt a malaise hovering like a dark cloud over Gotham. Something wasn't right. I feared that I had lost my ambitious drive. I felt untethered from any deeply anchored aspiration, and it was scary.

Like any hard-working, high-energy striving professional, I decided that I had to find a dream that mattered to work on. In desperation, I spent days trying to think of a new dream or else I feared I would live in a state of irrelevant mediocrity, going through the motions without any purpose. Each new idea failed to stick. For one reason or another I repeatedly kept ruling out options because I told myself they simply wouldn't work. Despite being a self-proclaimed striver committed to seeking many different forms of success, I couldn't find any traction. Anywhere.

Worse yet, I started to believe that my next twenty-five years would be void of an aspirational dream to pursue.

After a listless week, I finally caught myself out of the free fall. My experience reached out its hand to save me from ignominy. One thought occurred: Is the problem that I don't have a dream worth fighting for, or is the problem that my own personal demons are creeping up from my subconscious to hold me back and keep me shackled to my current reality?

Life throws us many curve balls. Some seem random; others, in the end, we find out were self-induced. Are demons circuit breakers installed for safety purposes? Or can our demons actually serve us?

An executive coach I was once working with at the time, Delynn Copley, once told me that our ways (good and bad) help us get to where we are today. But sometimes we need to evolve beyond those ways (and change/adapt) to get down the road further. In other words, be willing to embrace, and prepare for, change! To achieve career or economic independence, we have to recognize one simple, yet profound reality: **Change is inevitable. More than that, it's required.** We need to change to evolve. To continually adapt to the times, the situation, and to remake ourselves based on our inventory of skills and experiences.

However, beware. Our demons will evolve along the way as well. Resistance (demons surfacing and pushing back on our taking action on our dreams) never goes away. Resistance is friction; friction creates heat. Heat fuels the fire and frees us to make our dreams a reality.

I posit that the superhero Batman had his dreams and demons. He dreamed of a safer city where citizens could enjoy life without being undermined by the constant threat of crime. Yet, he often wondered if he, a mere mortal, could make a difference. He had to embrace his dream and manage his demons so he could succeed at elevating his potential.

Dream While Facing Demons

What is a dream? I define it as a desire for a specific and particularly personal and intended future, which I will discuss in more detail in the next chapter. How about a demon? It surfaces when we (potentially) mischaracterize a current reality (as a fear) and further compound the misperception into an uncertain future. This mischaracterization then seems to paralyze us and hold us back.

The truth is that if we stopped and took inventory of our journey to date, with various ups and downs to reminisce about, we all could see periods of our lives where we indeed were living our dream—and had an edge over our demons. The reverse we can see was also true; our demons can keep us from our dreams.

I generally believe I am a happy and positive person. I have been living my dream. And I continue to believe I am fully capable of being a valuable contributor to society and those around me until I die (another twenty-five years, I can only hope). But my demons started to rise when I consider my messages in this book: Have I really achieved what I wanted to achieve? To whom am I relevant to? Are my experiences, skills, talents, and assets useful any longer? Is my run over? Is it time to go home? Retire? Am I simply no longer of any good use to anyone?

We can be launched by our dreams or grounded by our demons. The question then becomes, do we have the self-awareness to turbocharge our dreams and take action while fighting off our demons? This can be the difference between success or failure.

The good news is that we get to decide what our own definition of success can look like.

Many people will say that they dream of accumulating wealth yet have no real idea what they'll do with it. I'd argue that what most of us really want is to find the love of our lives, our soul mate, build a family that exudes our shared belief system, afford a home and a nice car or two, take vacations, pay for healthcare and education, buy gifts for our loved ones, and, once in a blue moon, buy toys. Hasn't it already been said that the difference between men and boys is the price of their toys? That's a perfectly valid dream.

Some dream of changing the world for the better. That's a good one too. Maybe you dream of a promotion or a new career. The fun part about dreams is that there is no "sell by date" or limit to their numbers. And it's fair and okay that our dreams also can change over time as we evolve.

Our childhood dreams drastically changed when we hit puberty and just dreamed of having a date for the prom. That's okay too. The point? Dare to dream without holding onto your demons. Conversely, face your demons while holding onto your dreams.

* * *

Remember when Batman was surrounded by bad guys who were capable of giving him a beating? Instead of risking injury, he reached for his utility belt and pulled out a gun that could shoot out a grappling hook. He pointed it up and fired off a hook attached to a monofilament wire that, once secured at a higher elevation, would activate a powerful motorized-pulley system that gave him a quick ascent to a higher point, such as a rooftop, to escape the threat. (And gain a different perspective!)

We need a metaphorical grappling hook to carry us higher than our demons. We need tools to overcome resistance.

Self-awareness is the place to start.

To rise above our demons, it's imperative we learn to identify them.

For example, the most common fear shared by most humans is public speaking. I'd guess one of the demons could be fear of embarrassment. Forgetting what to say. Saying something wrong. Stage fright! Nobody likes to be embarrassed, but now that we identify the fear, we can face it. And prepare for it.

For some reason, we humans gravitate toward worst-case scenarios without really thinking it through. You may have heard that fear can be an acronym for **F**alse **E**xpectations **A**ppearing **R**eal. To counter this, I believe we need to scrutinize fear and reduce it by ballooning it into parody.

Is being embarrassed irreparable? No. Will being embarrassed provide valuable experience? Absolutely. Will the audience truly shame you? Probably not. I've found that others appreciate the speaker who unintentionally fails and does something embarrassing.

Sometime between 2006 and 2009, when my company at the time, Cohen Financial, was the debt platform for Colliers International, an external consultant and I developed a training program to help salespeople of various products and services with personal positioning and cross-training. Over thirty-nine months, Stew Gall (with Shirlaws, an international consulting firm) and I led fifty-six sessions and trained more than 1,100 commercial real estate professionals, thus creating more than $67 million of newfound revenue. As part of the training, each participant (groups of a dozen or so) had to stand in front of the room and share their "Red Shirt" explaining why they offered a unique selling proposition. I treasured those days, the people I met, the stories we shared.

On one training day, a gentleman stood up to present. He sputtered a few words and then literally keeled over and passed out. He hit the floor. We all rushed to help him up. He gathered his wits and ran from the room. The guy was so embarrassed. Rightly so.

How did the group respond? We took a break, came back, and started again. Eventually, our colleague returned to the program, watched a few of his colleagues progress through their Red Shirt presentations, and he asked for the floor to try once again. I have never seen energy in a room change so fast and form a supportive shield for a colleague like this.

When he finished his presentation, the group erupted into cheers. Not only was his Red Shirt the best presentation this group had seen, but all of us were taken and inspired by his courage to fight through his anxiety around stage fright.

It takes courage to be on stage, and everyone knows it. They pull for you, instead of pulling you down. The next time you speak publicly, confidence goes up. Now, if you let this demon hold you back, you'll never get on the stage and never evolve into the speaker you want to be. This reminds me of a story.

My son Jared was in kindergarten or first grade, and he came home excited to tell his mom and me that he had an opportunity to speak in front of the class at school. Before Jared could finish his statement, his mom blurted out, "Wait.

What? On stage? What if you don't look right? Sound right? Say something stupid? Embarrass yourself."

I was stunned. As a confident public speaker, I said to her, "Honey, you are scaring the crap out of me. Poor Jared, why destroy his fantasy with *your* reality?" Jared's mom meant well, she did. But she is afraid of public speaking and her demons took over, and without thinking she was just passing her demons on to her son. (By the way, though she struggled with stage fright, she actually was a very effective speaker at her kids' bar mitzvahs and wedding.)

It's unfortunate, but often resistance to our aspirations (triggering our demons) comes in the form of those people closest to us. Family. We love them, and they love us. Out of that love, they can say things they think will help protect us. Maybe they just don't share our vision and instead pile their demons on top of us to scare us into a holding pattern, even unintentionally. It's normal to experience resistance. Now you know the threat, and that's half the battle.

In the 1993 movie *Dragon, The Bruce Lee Story*, Bruce Lee asked his sifu (teacher) why his own father put him into martial arts at such a young age. The sifu said, "Your father loved you. He was a superstitious man, and as such, felt the devil would come after you. He wanted you to be skilled to defend yourself. However, as with most parents, he never understood that as a parent if you do not tame your demons, you will pass your fears on to your children. His fear was the devil!"

I was on a daddy-son trip with Jared. He couldn't have been more than four or five. We were in bed watching this Bruce Lee movie. When I heard this line spoken, I put the video on pause and made a note. The next day, Jared, ever so aware, asked me why I stopped the movie and made a note. I repeated the comment and told him it was an "aha moment" for me as a parent. I shared that my father had his demons (that he was either unaware of or in self-denial about) that he unwittingly had passed down to me. I told Jared that I needed to be better than that and conquer my demons, so I didn't pass them on to him.

Great parenting moment, right? Kinda proud of myself.

Well, a few days later we got home, and Jared ran out of the car to see his mom. Mom, excited to see her son, was racing to hug him home. Just before contact, Jared stopped short, looked at his mom, and asked, "Mommy, are you working on your demons, so you don't pass them on to me?"

You guessed it. A fight ensued between Mom and Dad. She wrongfully concluded I was talking bad about her in front of her son. Oh well. No good deed goes unpunished.

F.E.A.R. Can Be Productive

At their core, demons are baked in F.E.A.R. Yet could this mean fear is a liar? Actually, fear can be a productive emotion, if sorted properly. It's cloaked in an opportunity to breed courage and, ultimately, confidence as we push ourselves to chase skills, to drive growth, and to make progress. Fear of failure is another demon that keeps us stuck in our tracks. But failure is a given. Further, I don't think failure is a demon. Being paralyzed because you *fear* failure is a demon. I think the only failure that is a true failure is quitting rather than getting back up from a failure.

There is a cute vignette in one of the Dark Knight movies where Bruce Wayne as a little boy falls into a well on the property. His father finds him and rescues him while saying "Bruce, why do we fall down? So we can learn to get up again!"

If we don't fail, we will never grow.

Failure is required to succeed because we learn what not to do and we evolve. My point is that fear of failure could be a productive motivation, as long as the fear doesn't freeze you from taking action, any action, toward your desire to grow. Complacency would be the demon that results from fearing failure.

As a young professional, I worked for my dad's mortgage banking business. As a child, prior to my professional years, I thought my dad was larger than life. I had taken for granted that he had a grandiose persona. Then I went to work for him and saw just how human he was. He'd yell at people inappropriately (wait, is there an appropriate way to yell at someone?), make questionable decisions, and take bad decisions on the chin. My dad professed that we should "make the deal or learn the lesson!"

He generally owned up to his mistakes and became financially successful. Success aside, working for my dad often scared me. My aspirations, tools at hand, my education, and life experiences differed from my dad's, as they should be. I didn't want to be held back by my dad's aspirations and views of the world.

Neither right nor wrong, over time I came to accept how different my dad's dreams were to mine. He wanted a local business that supported how he wanted to live. I wanted a global business that protected and grew shareholder value. The hard part was that neither of us was attuned to this subconscious, but brewing, conflict. My dad started in anger to ask me, "What's wrong with how I run the business?"

Looking back now, I can see the demon in his question. He

fed off the authority to do it his way without disturbing his lifestyle or being challenged. In a manner of speaking, he created a domain where he could dominate. In truth, no one likes being told how to do their job. Worse yet, telling your father, a real-life, risk-taking, successful entrepreneur, that you didn't value everything he valued? Not good. Especially when it stood in the way of my vision.

All I wanted was the freedom to make my own mistakes, instead of feeling that I was being forced to compromise my dreams. I was curious. I wanted more. I didn't know what, but this wasn't my life's dream. I didn't want to be constrained. I wanted to act on my professional curiosities and to see what was on the other side of the proverbial fence. (Note to the reader: This sense of being constrained – held back by another - has stayed with me for my entire career. Working for my dad was merely the first of many points in my career where I felt "ants in my pants" and heard the siren call me for change on my journey.)

Although our dreams and demons differed, I knew for a fact that I didn't want to end up like a successful competitive contemporary of my dad who in his mid-sixties still worked for his ninety-three-year-old father who came into the office every single day to tell him what he wanted him to do. I didn't want to be told what to do, then or now. I felt the pull of freedom.

* * *

You could think about the path to achieving your dreams, while facing your demons, like Tarzan swinging from vine to vine. If he let his demons win, he would still be hanging onto one vine for dear life. After all, the risk of letting go of the vine we are swinging on before grasping the next vine is a scary proposition.

At some point in all our lives, I believe we need to take a clue from Tarzan. And I'm not talking about beating our chests while yodeling. Tarzan learned he had to let go of the vine he was on in order to get to where he wanted to end up. Yes, the freedom of mid vine flight is an exceptional rush and indeed necessary. If Tarzan had allowed himself to be crippled by a demon for fear of falling, he couldn't really reach for the next vine. However, instead of hanging onto one vine, he reached for, extended himself, and grabbed onto what he fervently believed was the next part of his journey for progress.

That's what I want for you: the skills, tools, and confidence to let go of one vine as you reach for another, regardless of the current climate in your life. Think about your own journey. How many times in your past have you yearned for a new path yet clung safely to your existing position? How many times have you found yourself unwilling to let go and try something new? How many times have you had in your grip two different vines, paralyzed and unwilling to let go and move on?

When my kids neared college age, I bought a couple of reference books about colleges and put them on the coffee table near the TV. I never said a word. I hoped that in a moment of boredom, they'd pick up one of the books and flip through to find a school that caught their attention.

After a while, I asked Jared, "Where do you think you want to go to college?" Quietly, seemingly facing unprepared defeat, he moped back to his room. Later, he would tell me his dream for college: "I just want to be happy." Clever actually.

He ended up searching online for the "happiest colleges," and an article in the *Washington Post* popped up with a metric that listed the fifty happiest colleges. From this list, he narrowed his search for college and made his selection. I applaud him to this day for letting go of what he believed met my expectation for finding a school. Instead, he grabbed onto a vine that took him on a new journey of self-awareness and making his own decisions. (And making his own mistakes, as life taught him that happiness is generated internally, not externally.) Fast-forward fifteen years. He is one of my teachers and mentors.

* * *

I come across a lot of people, young professionals included, who haven't been able to articulate their dreams. They're stuck like I described myself at the beginning of this chapter. Sometimes I find it helpful to re-frame dreams and demons. Think of dreams as aspirations, and demons as resistance or friction to the aspiration.

Answering the question, "What or who do you aspire to be (and by when)?" can help redefine your dreams into values, character, and qualities that breed excellence. Aspirations are easier vines to grab onto. As a form of pull energy (a concept I explore further in the next chapter), aspirations can take you higher and further than trying to push yourself with mere strong will.

If you aspire to be a better tennis player, then you have to play against better players. Clearly, you are going to get your ass kicked game after game. That's resistance, which can propel your game forward. The same is true at your work or in other areas of your life. Find someone smarter, further along on their journey, or better than you at a particular skill or job and spend time with them. You may resist this suggestion, fearing they may think you're a fraud or merely not worthy of their time.

The fact remains, you can't grow in a vacuum. I come back to this theme in subsequent chapters. We all need to be shown how to get what we want and take on the attributes of those we respect and who have been there before.

You don't need a dream board or vision board. You need a dream team of advisers and mentors who stimulate your aspirations. When you listen and learn from them, you create human leverage for yourself. With this leverage and swing momentum, you can catapult yourself into another realm of opportunity that was never thought available before.

The resistance to human leverage can be self-defeating thoughts (demons), blaming others, and a lack of experience or confidence. But a dream team can help you navigate around or through these demons. Just like dreams change, so do demons. So, the key to this entire discussion is learning to be self-aware and have the courage to face your demons. I have found that often demons seem like monsters in the closet. But if you open the closet door, you'll see there's nothing there.

* * *

By now, you might be asking, "Okay, Jack, what's your dream?"
Freedom.

I have always cherished freedom for myself and, as such, protected freedom for others. Freedom as a context has propelled me to acquire skills, accumulate experiences, and develop relationships. All of this fosters for me financial, emotional, and physical independence.

Over the past few years, I've been working for ArrowMark Partners, a $24 billion investment management firm, where I have been spending fifty+ hours a week as a managing director. But during the summer of 2023, my colleagues allowed me to follow a dream to have the freedom to write this book. I needed, and they gave me, more bandwidth for myself. In return, I reduced my base pay by 40 percent so that I would feel I wasn't taking advantage of their generosity.

Unfortunately, my demons started creating resistance. As opposed to courageously using that extra time to start writing, I started to wonder, do I really have enough in the tank? Would anyone really care what I had to say? Nobody's going to buy a book written by me. Did I just make a stupid decision that cost me thousands of dollars in income? What was I thinking?

But I grabbed onto a new vine and decided to create some human leverage for me. I found a literary arts firm that could find a writing partner to help me get my concepts and teachings down on paper. Then I took the required action. To hell with my demons, I thought.

Demons and resistance come in so many forms. As part of my freedom context, back in 1984 I learned to be a pilot. Over time, I evolved from a basic private pilot to becoming instrument-rated, upgrading to a commercial license, to becoming multi-engine rated, and, eventually, earned an Airline Transport Pilot's license and type ratings that certified me to fly various types of jets. Although twice I took many years off from flying, I have always loved the *freedom* experienced in flight.

Having gone back to aviation as a recreational pilot in July of 2021, I decided I wanted to buy another plane. Over time, of course, I got carried away and went way over budget with my purchase. After I committed to the purchase in September 2022, I would routinely wake up in the middle of the night absolutely petrified that I was going to go broke. My demons awoke. Who was I to think that I could afford a plane like this one? What if I outlived my savings and ended up poor and homeless because of this folly?

Fast-forward to a break I took from writing this book to attend a three-day flight training in Wichita, Kansas. The sessions were challenging, and I got frustrated at times, but I had a blast. Afterward, I flew home at an altitude of 40,000 feet as a single pilot in my jet. The thought occurred: How cool is this? There is no better feeling than to have learned a new skill and be propelled across your landscape! Is there anything more freeing and independent than soaring above the clouds piloting your own aircraft? I'd earned this privilege and now could enjoy it. I'd left those demons at ground level.

I'm living my dream.

Now, what's your dream? Let's put some thought into that in the next chapter.

Quick Takes

- Change is inevitable. More than that, it's required. You can't grow in a vacuum.
- Dare to dream without holding onto your demons. Conversely, face your demons while holding onto your dreams.
- We must identify our demons to overcome them.
- Fear can be the most productive emotion. It can be liberating as, and if, you can learn to work with it.

Bringing It All Together

My overarching context is personal freedom. The idea for the book, the context for the Freedom Frameworks, is how these principles, as tools, can occupy space in your utility belt and enable you to cultivate the kind of freedom that enables you to pursue your dreams and overcome your demons. Freedom is a mindset that I fervently believe everyone can cultivate and embody. All you need are the tools—skills, experiences, relationships (and maybe savings)—to empower you.

2

The Foundation

Winter break from college arrived. My daughter, Lindsay, who was home for the holiday, invited some friends to our house for a little "pre-gaming" before they headed out to a party. Over the course of the evening, I asked one of her friends, a young lady who was in her senior year at Pomona College, "So, what are you going to do when you graduate?"

"Mr. Cohen, I don't have any idea," she said laughing. "I'm an English major at a liberal arts school, so we'll just have to wait and see."

Instantly, I felt a pang of guilt on behalf of my generation of parents who somehow managed to convey to our kids that college education provided an express train to success. You may know this thinking: live in the right neighborhood, go to the right school, do well in high school, which launches you to attend the right college, that in turn puts you in the right seat at the right company in the right industry that acts as your platform for wealth and fame. As if, through functional incrementalism, success was a linear journey to having everything you ever wanted.

Not all, but I'm guessing most, parents from my generation have misled their children about what success looks like and what it took to get there. Not intentionally, of course. Today's younger generation looks at what we have (and that they have derivatively enjoyed and don't want to give up in search of their own independence) and wonder how we got there. Perhaps wrongly assuming our path was linear, short, without troughs in our journey, and filled with peaks that got higher and higher and higher as we progressed. But we know it was more of a zigzag with lots of ups and downs, trials, and failures.

The fact is, **it's 100 percent okay not to know what you want to do with your life.** There's always time to pivot as you move forward, and, eventually, clarity will be revealed. Since success is a moving target, and dreams can feel like intangible ideas far off in the future, this chapter offers some foundational frameworks. The rest of the book is built upon those frameworks, which are keys to achieving career and economic independence. Here they are:

- Be. Do. Have.
- Context vs. Content
- Begin with the End in Mind
- Intended Future, Current Reality, Transition Plan
- Outcome vs. Source Activities
- Pull vs. Push Energy

Admittedly, these are meaty concepts that may need to be read a few times, meditated on, and considered as you move forward in the book. However, these frameworks are essential to establishing your road map and knowing how to get to your destination—even if the destination keeps moving on you.

Before we establish the foundational frameworks, I want to start by pointing out the learning and skill acquisition process goes in stages. Why is this important? Because when you learn something, it takes time and practice until it becomes second nature. This growth process is called the four stages of competence, which originally appeared in a 1960 textbook written by three professors from New York University. It looks like this:

1. Unconsciously Incompetent: You don't know that you don't know about how to do something.
2. Consciously Incompetent: You know that you don't know how to do something.
3. Consciously Competent: You know how to do something, but it requires concentrated effort to get it done.
4. Unconsciously Competent: You know how, and execution on a skill becomes second nature. You need not think about it as you are in the flow.

Four Stages of Competence

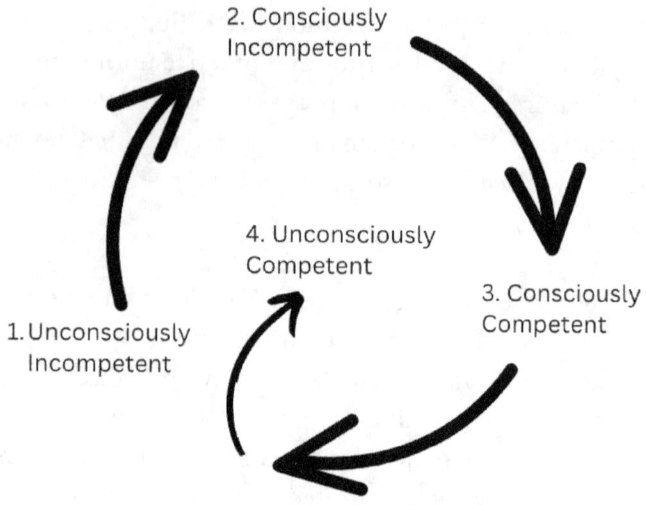

Figure 1

The four stages of competence help identify where you are in learning a new skill.

As we learn new skills (for example, a new technique in sports), gaining competence goes through these four stages.

A wake-up call exists for those attempting to learn something new inside or outside the classroom. To illustrate this, I'll often use a dry-erase board when I'm speaking to a group of young (and old) professionals. First, I draw a circle and say, "This circle represents everything you know." It's a small circle, so typically everyone laughs.

"What's outside this circle?" I ask next.

Usually, someone will answer, "What we don't know."

Then, I draw a second ring around the first one. "Okay then, what's outside this circle?" This usually stumps the room. Then, I'll clarify with something like, "I set you up, so let me give you the answer. The first circle is not what you know. It's what you *know* you know. The second circle is what *you know you don't know*." As I draw a big circle around the second ring, I add, "This third circle is where all the growth happens. *It's everything you didn't know you didn't know.*"

The 3 Rings

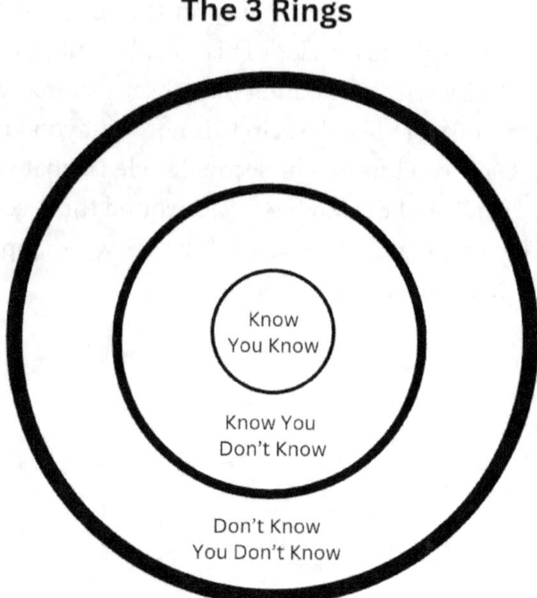

Figure 2

I use the three rings when speaking to groups to illustrate what you know you know and you know you do not know, as well as what you don't know you don't know.

Finally, I'll put a small dot right in the middle of the bull's-eye (borrowing again from Aleen Bayard). "This is your comfort zone. If you stay here and never learn how to be uncomfortable with growth, then you'll never experience all you wanted to be." I have found that all growth happens in the third ring. And the discomfort that you are feeling when you go from the small dot out to the third ring is essentially growth.

Comfort to Discomfort

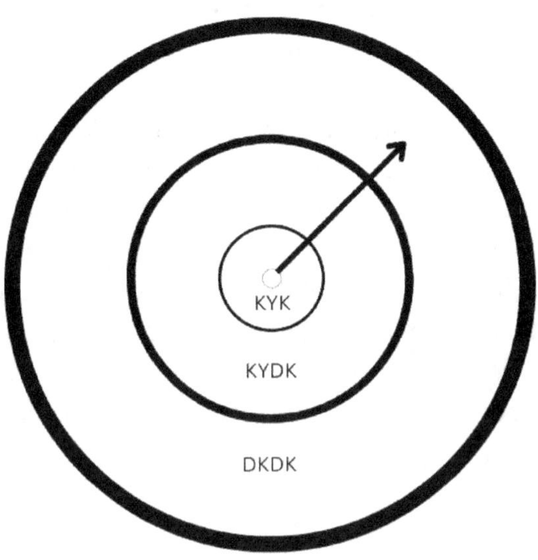

Figure 3

Growth occurs when moving from your comfort zone to areas of discomfort, which reflects learning things you never knew you didn't know.

I think that higher education sold college graduates a bill of goods. College education, contextually, is sold as expanding the first circle into the second, therefore consuming the second ring entirely. This, of course, is silly and misses the point of being a lifelong learner.

My goal is to move you along each of these stages, so that whatever you're doing, when a situation arises, you can immediately recall one of these frameworks and apply them to get the best outcome. I want to help optimize your skill set so you evolve into a more effective human being with more options and, ultimately, more freedom.

Beware: Failure is ahead. Whenever we start the learning process, we must look at failure differently. We learn from our mistakes. Author and former football coach Bill Walsh wrote, "I would never write anything that suggests the path to success is a continuum of positive, even euphoric experiences—that if you do all the right things everything will work out. Frequently it doesn't; often you crash and burn. This is part and parcel of pursuing and achieving very ambitious goals . . . Almost always, your road to victory goes through a place called failure."

Be. Do. Have.

Success is a variable, defined differently for everyone by everyone. In fact, I really don't think anyone has found an objective measurement for success. Making things more complicated, I think some see success in another, while that other may not agree about being successful themselves. I confess, I struggle with this. Sure, I have had some successful outcomes in my life. Maybe even at least one more than the failures that have piled up along my journey. However, I did not write this book believing that "I had arrived" as a success. At best, I am willing to concede that I am a caricature of what others believe to be a success.

To help set the foundation for your career dreams and aspirations, setting your sights on what success might look like for you, I offer the Be. Do. Have. code—which I believe was originally created by Werner Erhard. Basically, he stated that if we don't clarify for ourselves who/what we want to **be**, and then **do** the things to get us there, we will never **have** what we want.

Unfortunately, most believe the opposite is true: they think that if they **have** the right degree or amount of money, they can **do** the what they want (like getting a particular job), and then of course they would **be** happy.

However, let's turn this around by considering what—or who—you want to **be** (by when). Then, **do** the actions to get there until you **have** what you want.

The beauty is that it only takes an instant to decide what you want to be. (Oh, and you are, of course, free to change your mind, over and over and over again!) If you want to be an astronaut, then decide now and start acting like one. Get the education you need and work your way in that direction. You don't have to wait for NASA to agree with you, and eventually it may.

Context vs. Content

A guy goes up to a church under construction and sees three people building three of the brick walls. He asks the first worker, "What are you doing?"

The worker replies, "I'm building a wall."

Then he asks the second worker, "What are you doing?"

"I'm building a church," the worker says.

Then he asks the third worker, "What are you doing?"

The third worker says, "I'm building a house of God. When I am done, we can all come together and worship."

This story about the church bricklayers is also another example of context. Each worker answered the question with a different context to the same content (laying bricks). All of them are correct, but each brought different perspectives to the same job. The first was focused on his job/task, the second was focused on his career as a bricklayer. The third was focused on making the world a better place. Which answer was most motivating for you? (Which is why your "why" is the mother of all contexts.)

One framework I use repeatedly is that **context gives meaning to content.** I first learned the concept from Stew Gall, a professional business coach who worked for an international small business enterprise coaching firm called Shirlaws, years and years ago. It truly is a game changer. Yet, for some reason, folks (me included) struggle to grasp this concept. But when they do, it really sets the right foundation for further discussions.

When I say that context gives meaning to content, I can suggest a metaphor of the container and what we put in it. Context is the container. Content is what we pour into it. We need a context that is large enough to hold the content.

Content vs. Context

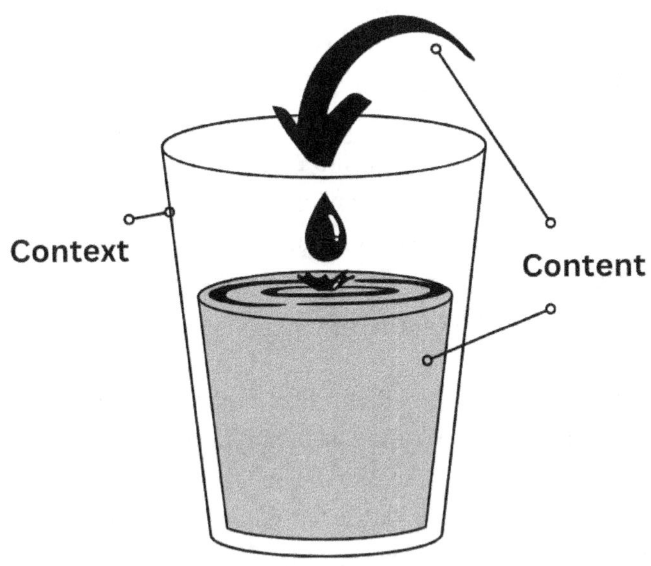

Figure 4

Confused? How about this? If you and I are standing on a dock protruding into a lake and I say, "bow," you will look to the front of the boat parked at the dock. If you and I, by comparison, have just given a presentation to an audience of adoring fans, and I say, "bow," you will bend at the waist. Context gives meaning to content. Bow is content. The dock or the stage gives the content proper context. The context lends meaning. The context is the container that holds our content.

Okay, grammar aside, how is this remotely relevant? Well, Albert Einstein once offered the idea, loosely translating here, that you cannot solve a problem at the level at which it was created. Rather, you need to go up a level and keep going up until you can solve the problem that created the problem in the first place. He was speaking of finding a higher context.

Let me share a real-life scenario when context gives meaning to content first clicked for me.

When I decided to leave my first marriage, it coincided with an effort to raise $80 million to expand our business, Cohen Financial. I wanted co-parenting in the divorce and didn't want an every-other-weekend kind of schedule. The time I saw my kids was one night during the week, every other weekend, and one weekend day on the weekend I didn't have my kids full-time.

In the meantime, the $80 million capital raise was, in part, to be used to buy other mortgage banking businesses across the country and unify them under the Cohen Financial brand. I was getting frazzled with the travel necessary to pull off our business expansion. I'd get on a plane to travel out to another city and fly back to meet my in-week parenting commitments or weekend coverage. As you'd expect, these responsibilities and stress of it all started to weigh heavily on me. I got really tired really fast. I started to exhibit burnout, frustration, and hostility.

One day, working with Stew Gall as my coach, he asked me a simple question: "Why are you going to such trouble?" The mother of all contexts is the answer to the question, "Why?" Why we are doing something actually gives us an understanding.

The point of answering Stew's "Why?" question was that all my pain and suffering was due to the content I was squeezing into my life. Travel here, there, anywhere. Grow a business. Be a father, husband. Stay in shape. Build new skills, etc.

However, if I could find a higher level of context, broader than just putting the capital to work building our business, maybe I could find greater meaning and make it more worthwhile. Or easier to withstand. It didn't take long for me to recognize the choice that I willingly made.

I decided that my context was parenting. I wanted to be the best dad that I could be. My context for parenting was to manufacture two things: memories and adults. And I couldn't do that remotely. If I really wanted to be THAT DAD, I had to be on-site, physically present, and arrange the rest of my activities around making memories with, and adults out of, my children.

This, of course, didn't reduce the burden of all my travel, but it did give me purpose and free me from complaining about the burden. Rather, in a weird way, it energized me because I was living my dream to expand the business as well as supporting my aspirations for the kind of dad I wanted to be.

As the Dalai Lama once put it, "Pain might be mandatory, but suffering is optional." I have personally found that holding the right context can alleviate a lot of suffering. Or, at a minimum, it could pull me through the suffering I couldn't avoid.

When I attempt to teach content versus context to business professionals, for some reason it takes time for the concept to take hold. All I can say is if you read and reread the explanation I've given, if you can relate to my divorced parenting burden, over time this concept that context gives meaning to content will click.

I have learned that when we get too caught up with the content in our lives, we may need to revisit, or redefine, our context holding the content. For example, if you want to own a business someday—the context—you may have to deal with working for someone else until you know how to launch out on your own—the content. But if you don't have the context set, you won't have the desire to pull yourself through the friction of your day-to-day misery—the content.

#BWEIM

Context, as a framework, and the mother of all "Why?" answers, segues nicely into another framework. If you can, why not begin with the end in mind (#BWEIM), a concept borrowed from Stephen Covey's book, *The 7 Habits of Highly Effective People*. Beginning with the end in mind can help set context. It also can direct your "BE."

By beginning with an end in mind, the outcome you seek can become a context to pull you forward. This is what I also often refer to as **pull energy**.

The next time you are in the gym, ask someone to put a 100-pound weight on the floor. Then, try pushing the weight across the floor. It's clumsy and hard, right? Now, try grabbing one end and pulling it. Which is easier? Pushing or pulling the weight across the floor?

Mechanically, the answer is pulling requires less energy and is more effective than pushing a heavy object. Ever see a horse pushing a cart? NEVER! Horses pull carts. Life is the same way. We need to be propelled by pull energy rather than push energy.

Back to the point, beginning with an end in mind, how we get there will, of course, require us to live in the content. I think it was the White Rabbit in *Alice in Wonderland* who said to Alice, "If you don't know where you're going, any road will get you there."

Let me offer another example of beginning with the end in

mind. When you think of taking a vacation sometime in the future, does it require any planning? Would you ever pack your bags, put all the contents in your car, and drive on vacation without knowing where you were going and what you were planning on doing? Of course not.

Instead, we need a destination to work backward from so we can pack only what we need. Then, we can answer questions like: Will it be warm or cold? Are we going to do passive or active activities? Is the destination near or far? Will we walk, bike, drive, or fly to the location? And what gear and clothes should we pack?

In life, and with our career choices, we also need to identify some destination, at least directionally. Yet, how often do we see young professionals who don't have a clue about their destination? If they do, they often have the aperture of the lens tuned too narrowly.

Enter another Freedom Framework: As you consider #BWEIM, I encourage you to fantasize about your intended future.

Intended Future, Current Reality, Transition Plan

While participating in an industry association board meeting, where we attempted to reset the association's long-term strategy, Debbie McAneny, who served at the time as the head of commercial real estate lending at John Hancock Life Insurance Company, introduced me to the current reality, intended future framework. Since learning the framework from Debbie decades ago, I have repurposed this framework for use in strategic planning, problem solving, PowerPoint presentations, career planning, and even for setting out my own transition plans in life. Let me walk you through it.

Take out a piece of paper and create three vertical columns, with the middle column twice as wide as the columns on the right and the left. Title the column on the right Intended Future.

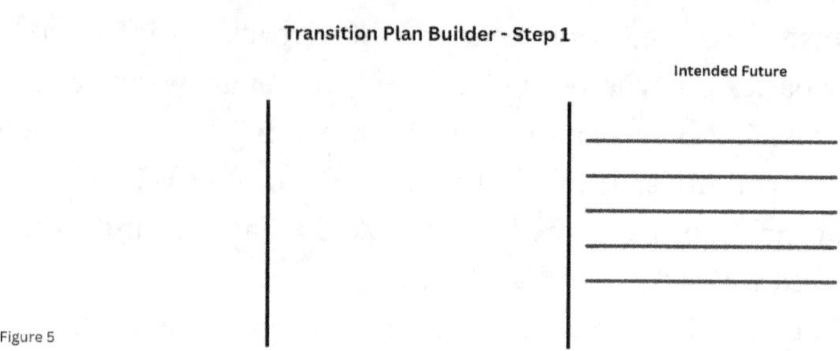

Step 1 is to list/inventory what we identify/dream about elements of our Intended Future.

Now, think about and pick a point in time in the future. This could be three months, three years, ten years, or thirty years out. The duration doesn't matter. It's just a point in time and an exercise. If you are struggling picking the point in time and if you are stuck even at the beginning of the exercise, let us steal a concept from author Simon Sinek, from his book *The Infinite Game,* where he talks about moving the goalposts as far away as you need to unstick yourself. (Pick a time in the future far, far away.)

A properly envisioned intended future can create the lift of pull energy. As such, I encourage you to fantasize. In fact, I insist that you fantasize. That is indeed the point. I find that since your intended future is at this point pure fantasy ("man plans, while God laughs"), when using this framework, you need to pick a time in the week when you are at your most serene, fantastical best. To begin, maybe you need to know your biorhythms, which I address in chapter 7, but let me explain here.

For me, the best time to work on the intended future portion of the framework would be after dinner on a Friday night when I am alone with my thoughts. Or it could be Sunday morning after a good night's sleep and a hard workout and active Saturday. (This is what I mean by knowing your own personal biorhythms.)

Now, pick that future point in time (duration out into the future), close your eyes, and dream yourself to that intended future. Then, open your eyes and take inventory of all that you envision around you. What elements of that future do you see? List them until you are exhausted. What do you see around you when you peek into your specific intended future? Be limitlessly specific. Include material possessions, the job, the club, the home(s), vacations, friends, and family—things you envision actually doing in this fantasy. (At some level that environment that you fantasize about is indeed an outcome you seek.)

Does your intended future include an ex-partner, a new spouse, a girlfriend/boyfriend (all three?), kids, a dog, a plane, a set of skills, prestige, a location to live, another language to be able to speak fluently, or an ability to juggle chainsaws? Or do you simply have an intended future where you own enough income-producing assets that give you monthly cash flow you can rely upon so that you don't have to work but can hang out with your fourteen grandchildren? Or play endless rounds of golf? It doesn't matter.

List everything you can imagine in that intended future. Be

silly in your comprehensiveness of this list. Then put this piece of paper away, for at least a week.

The last time I did this exercise was one Christmas vacation with my family in Mexico. Every year over Christmas vacation, I try to assess how I did on my annual goals in order to recalibrate my journey for the year to come. At some level, I attempt to choose context words to guide me year to year. While I don't remember which pre-pandemic vacation I did the intended future fantasy, I do remember marveling about how well my father managed his financial independence.

My dad passed February 24, 2022. He was ninety-three. His passing set for me a milestone I wanted to achieve (#BWEIM): I wanted to live to ninety-four. So, I picked my intended future date out to my mid-nineties. One of my goals in life is to be married fifty years to Nancy. As she was my second marriage, as we came together when we were forty-five, I need to last till age ninety-five. So my fantasy indeed included Nancy, our vibrant marriage, physical fitness, mobility creating physical freedom, economic independence (so I didn't have to be put in a nursing home), board and advisory positions where I could continue to mentor young professionals, constant visits by my four children, their spouses, and their kids (so I couldn't grow up to become a curmudgeon), and yes, some form of involvement in aviation.

Back to *your* exercise—

A week or so later, you need to sit down and do an inventory of your current reality. Minding your biorhythms, you need to pick a different time or day in the week. To accomplish this next task, pick a time in the week when you are your most cold-hearted, calculating, and unemotional in your assessments. It's time for "just the facts, ma'am!" For me, it's 6:00 a.m. Monday morning when I'm prepared to face the week. Retrieve that piece of paper you started and add Current Reality to the top of the left column.

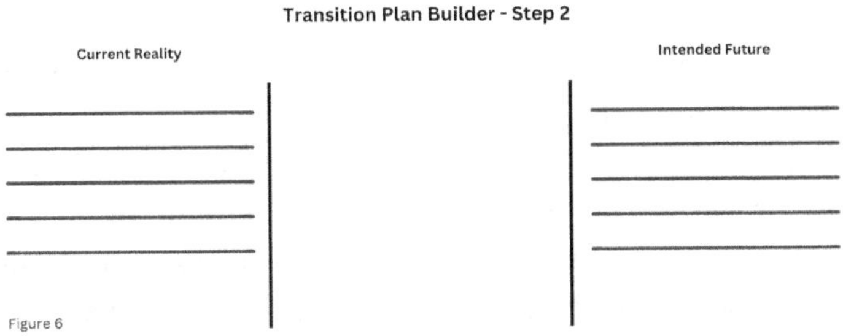

Transition Plan Builder - Step 2

Current Reality

Intended Future

Figure 6

Step 2 is to list what your Current Reality looks like.

This is the time where you don't fantasize, nor do you close your eyes. Rather, look around you and take an honest inventory of everything in your life. What's going on for you? Do you have close friends? Are you pleased with your partner? Your job? Your path? Are you overworked, underpaid, confused, possess too much debt, or not enough net worth? Are you out of shape, need to lose weight, stuck in unhealthy relationships?

This is a time for radical candor with yourself. Inventory it all. And in that inventory don't just beat on yourself with the negatives. Inventory the good stuff too—where you live, who you spend time with, what you love to spend time doing. Once complete, then put the piece of paper away for at least another week.

A week or so later, pick a time in the week when you are more balanced in your perspectives. Maybe it's midweek when the pressures of the early week have worn off and your sights are set on the weekend.

Then pull out the same piece of paper with the three columns, and what do you see? If you stare at what you see on the right and left columns, can you find a pattern(s)? As you look left and right at your current reality and intended future, what you should see is a gap.

Step 3 becomes the transition plan for bridging the gap between your current reality and your intended future. This is where the action plan, the real value of the exercise, comes into play as you inventory the activities to get from your current reality to your intended future. (This transition plan becomes the source activities.)

Transition Plan Builder - Step 3

Current Reality	Bridge the Gap	Intended Future

Figure 7

Step 3 involves bridging the gap between your current reality and your intended future. This becomes the transition plan and related activities.

If, by way of example, you decided that your intended future included living and working in Portugal. In your current reality, you realized you could not speak any language other than English. Obviously, you will conclude that between now and then (the time of your intended future) you will obviously need to learn Portuguese. An action plan is now needed and begins to develop. Where can you learn Portuguese? At a local community college? Online? An app? A tutor? You get the idea.

By imagining an intended future, and by assessing a current reality, you can begin to tie those two columns together with a transition plan designed to bridge the gap. By focusing on an intended future, you have a direction. Tying the two columns together, you can create common sub contexts, and those contexts become a collection of action plans for you to execute over time. The time it takes to reach your destination is now set.

Outcome vs. Source Activities

When I teach people about time management, I often find folks confused between activity and progress. It seems to me that everyone thinks they are busy. Busy no doubt, however I ask, to what end? The difference then between activity and progress is that progress is activity toward an endgame (#BWEIM)—an outcome.

It is here that we need to underscore the distinction between outcome and source activities. Again, I find, like with context vs. content, smart business professionals continue to confuse outcomes with the source activities necessary to achieve the outcomes related to their intended futures. Maybe it's because most of us live our lives, have our arguments, fight or support our wars, all in content. But you can **be** an outcome; you have to **do** source activities in order to **have** what you want.

Recently retired college football coach, Nick Saban, talks about "The Process." Nick Saban has won more college football championships than any other coach in history. By a lot! Did you also know that never, not one day during the season, does Coach Saban talk about winning a college football championship. That's right. None of the coaches ever talk about the desired outcome. Instead, they can be a winner if they do the work to have the championship.

Rather, Saban teaches that the prize, the championship, the goal, the outcome is simply a matter of doing your job. Day to day, play to play, game to game, do your job as well as you can. The process, the day-to-day efforts one puts in, is everyone's source activity.

Source activity leads to outcome. With a clearly defined desired outcome (aka goal, target, #BWEIM, or intended future), the source activities for the transition plan materialize rather quickly. However, without a clearly defined outcome, to hold the context, source activities can send you to a completely different destination. Think of the airline pilot. If their destination is not locked in, all the source activities it takes to fly a plane will never help them land in the desired location.

In life, the money we earn is an outcome from taking a particular job and doing the work hired to do that role. The job is the source activity that leads to buying a house—another outcome. Let me try that again: Most think making money to spend is an outcome. I posit we have merged source and outcome activities and confused them. The job done well, doing the work, is the source activity. Creating value for the employer is an outcome for our employer but another source activity for us. Getting that raise, that bonus, then becomes an outcome. Another outcome could be a promotion, a title change, new and improved responsibilities. Which, down the road, just might allow us to take a special vacation, learn a new language, buy a house, take flying lessons, pick up golf, or maybe even buy a plane.

Who am I to challenge Nick Saban, college football's GOAT? With no NCAA championships on my resume, where I differ from the great coach is that I recognize that an outcome focused upon creates pull energy and can provide context, which gives meaning to the content of our daily lives and those source activities.

Pull Energy vs. Push Energy

As I said earlier, we live our lives in content mode, working daily on source activities. Too many folks live in content mode and focus on the activities they feel define a successful outcome. I beg to differ. For me, I want to clearly define the outcome I seek. Can I paint for myself a clear picture of what a good outcome looks like? Can I get a better understanding from my boss as to how they will use the end product I create with the completion of a task?

By beginning with the end in mind, I can be lifted by the pull energy that my future self or future destination creates. It also works to define all my activities as making progress or failing to make progress.

How many of us suffered through a tough week of finals, or a rough patch at work, singularly focused on the freedom we will experience when it was over, and we were on summer break or a vacation? The concept is the same: The pull energy creates lift. It literally pulls us through the crap we need to get through.

You ask, what if I don't know where I am going or what I want to be? In my experience folks confuse what they want to be (outcome) with how they will get there (source activities).

They also confuse the job or role with the elements that make up the environment around the role that they aspire to with the job, title, and compensation package.

* * *

Before ending this chapter with my Quick Takes, I want to share a powerful moment in my life to recall when you finally get to be what you hoped, or get to your intended future, or arrive at your outcome. This story comes from little Jack Cohen, age thirteen, seventh grade.

Maybe you know me, or maybe you think you know me from reading this book. You might envision a Jack Cohen with a big mouth constantly sharing his opinions, whether asked for or not. I joke that I am "often wrong, but never in doubt!" That was true even in seventh grade.

One day during the school year, my class was treated to a substitute teacher for a few weeks. She and I had our moments. On her last day, she gave me a book.

"What's this?" I asked.

"Just read it," she said. "I think you will enjoy it."

I don't remember the name of the book or what it was about. But the book ended with a poem that I typed up and have kept in my wallet ever since—fifty-four years and counting:

When you get what you want in your struggle for self; and the world makes you king for a day. Just go to the mirror and look at yourself and see what that man has to say. For it isn't your father or mother or spouse whose judgment upon you must pass. The fellow whose verdict counts most in your life is the one staring back from the glass.

— Peter Dale Wimbrow Sr., Excerpt from The Guy In the Glass

I wish I knew who that substitute teacher was or remembered her name. She did me a great service by first understanding me, and then teaching me a lesson I would think about for my entire life. A true mentoring moment. I bow and say with appreciation, "Thank you."

Quick Takes

- Train to become unconsciously competent in your skill sets.
- The foundation to all the frameworks is Be. Do. Have, which will get you further than Have. Do. Be.
- "Context" gives meaning to "Content."
- Begin with the end of mind. Envision your intended future. Record your current reality. Build your transition plan.
- Determine what outcomes you'd like, then go after the source activities.

Bringing It All Together

These foundational frameworks are interrelated and take time for you to become unconsciously competent at them. Even longer to become unconsciously competent in using all of them. Interchangeably.

Be. Do. Have. starts with Be. I start from the be of being free to be who I want to be (responsibly).

Our Be is a context of our intended future that we want to envision so that we can begin with the end in mind. #BWEIM creates pull energy for us that gives us lift and propels us to work through our source activities that represent the transition plan for what we do day to day, living our lives in content, to get where we want to go.

All of these frameworks allow me to live my professional and personal life better, faster, and with more effectiveness in my journey for professional and personal freedom. I hope these foundational frameworks enable you to cultivate the kind of freedom that enables you to pursue your dreams.

3

Know the Lay of Your Land

Bruce Wayne knew the city of Gotham was in trouble. Crime, corruption, and lawlessness were on the rise. He knew every nook and cranny of the region, and most of the main players. His vision was to make a difference in the city where he lived, and he would leverage his own money, relationships, and skills to make it happen. Without any of this, he'd never become the Caped Crusader. He'd remain just a wealthy man without a purpose.

Stealing from this metaphor, we, too, need to know the lay of the land. In this case, I'm talking about types of businesses, trends, and influences that affect industry at large. If we don't know these aspects, then we need to identify what we want and can do. And, if we don't know that, we need to start with getting a job and zigzagging our way to figure it out over time.

With a sense for the type of business you want to work for, and the ability to see trends coming and spot influences that would create opportunity, you'll be able to find stepping-stones to where you want to be in five, ten, and twenty years down the road. But if you go blindly into an area, and in a business without a sense for relevant trends, then your survival is largely dependent on the will of your employer and economy.

However, in many cases, identifying these kinds of external influences comes over time. In other words, it's not the end of the world if you don't know what industry you want to work in, what trends are affecting its future, or what other influences may impact that business. In fact, it may be more imperative to know the individual lay of *your* land so you can develop your skill sets, regardless of the industry, to get where you want to be. As we grow our skill sets, experiences, and relationships, the external lay of the land will become more and more evident.

Career Growth Is More of a Zigzag, Not a Linear Path

My son Wyatt is an example of someone who didn't know what he wanted to be, do, or have. He didn't know the lay of the land anywhere, nor what value he could bring to an organization. But over time, he figured it out. Here's how.

He graduated with a degree in theater. He's the most fun person at any gathering. He can do a standing back flip. He has a magnetic personality. But how can he monetize those skills? How does he add value to an organization? Because doing a standing back flip doesn't add much value to an organization unless he wants to be a circus clown. But he can certainly leverage his personality to find both happiness and fulfillment.

Wyatt's journey started in New York after he finished formal theater training, where he would skateboard from Brooklyn to Manhattan. He had reached an age where I couldn't carry him on my insurance anymore, so I told him he needed a job that provided the benefit of health insurance. Something about the word *insurance* caught his attention, so he found a job opportunity to work with an insurance broker. It didn't take him long to realize he didn't want to work for that guy. He started to get a feel for the lay of his land. He kept looking.

The gold standard for life insurance is Northwestern Mutual. You guessed it. Wyatt found a job working at Northwestern Mutual (not an easy hill to climb). Their sales training is known to have the most prescriptive set of source activities that simply provide the most relied upon success for hitting sales targets. The job required him to make 200 phone calls per week, schedule a particular number of meetings, and learn a bunch of information that he had no passion for.

While he loved the calls and meetings and people interaction of the selling process, he's a creative, an actor, and skateboarder, so it wasn't a good fit. Although the position paid well, according to him, the job sucked the life out of him.

In between jobs, he found a gig skateboarding in the background for a commercial produced by an advertising agency. He stuck around after the shoot, asked a bunch of questions about what they did, hustled a job offer, and joined them. He found that environment more aligned with his creative and energetic preferences, and he wound up writing copy and helping out at the ad agency for a while.

But the agency lost a big client and couldn't afford to keep him on. In the process, he learned what he definitely did not want to do. (See The Donut Approach later in this chapter.) He also learned he wanted face-to-face interaction to leverage his love of people and the effect his personality has on others.

Along the way, he met a woman who had a new premium, and luxury, American whiskey she brought to the US market. After one meeting, and having been so impressed with my son's personality, she offered him a job as brand ambassador. His role was to visit ninety-five restaurants around the city and report back how much of the product was being sold, what training was needed for the bartenders and owners, and ultimately what advice was required for vendors on how to sell more whiskey. He skated from one restaurant to another and ended up increasing sales.

Due to an internal power struggle in the company, his job was axed. During the process, he learned he's good at face-to-face, one-on-one selling, and through networking (the woman business owner who fired him introduced him to other colleagues), he also discovered a new passion: luxury wristwatches.

In Tarzan-like vine-to-vine travel, Wyatt networked introduction to introduction and combined his new passion for watches with his desire to do face-to-face sales with luxury items and started working at a beautiful retail store in downtown Manhattan. He excelled, to say the least. Wyatt's career is now off and running, and, more importantly, he finds his work is fulfilling. Eight months later, Wyatt had sold more than 120 luxury watches and has made a name for himself with clients and at the store, not to mention some pretty good money.

While attending multiple routine sales trainings with brands that came to the store, Wyatt would go up to the trainer afterward, chat the person up, and ask them out for coffee. Over time, as watch manufacturer sales representatives came in to educate the sales team about their brands and timepieces, Wyatt was exposed to many brands including one of the most exclusive luxury jewelers in the world—Jacob & Co.

The cheapest watch Jacob & Co. sells is $22,000. The most

expensive watch comes in at $7 million (or more by the time you read this). This kind of luxury is afforded by the wealthiest people in the world, among many recognizable celebrities.

After training, and a stop and chat, the Jacob & Co. rep invited Wyatt for an interview, which he passed with flying colors. Now at twenty-nine years old, Wyatt is an external sales rep based in NYC and traveling the world educating store sales reps, meeting with prospective purchasers, and selling these out-of-this-world watches along the way. Naturally, his income increased as well.

On his very first business trip to Dubai, he managed to get deposits on five watches totaling $4 million in selling price. Since then, he's been to Miami, Chicago, LA, and Switzerland, all on a company credit card. And another $1 million of watches sold.

While I'm extremely proud of Wyatt's progress, the point is that his career route was more of a zigzag than a straight line. He acquired skills, accumulated experiences, and developed relationships. Each experience gave him more insight into what he liked and disliked. Now, his career will open him further to people, places, and luxury he never imagined. Not bad for a theater student whose best skill out of school was improv and being able to do a standing back flip.

The Four-Step Framework (for Commercial Real Estate Careers)

While I was speaking at the University of Illinois a number of years ago, in support of the real estate department, one of the students raised his hand and told me that he wanted to be a developer.

I told him, "Terrific. But I'm curious, how did you come to

that conclusion? What do you actually know about being a developer?"

His answer: "I want to be rich." (Note the outcome sought.)

In his defense, he was probably twenty years old and had taken fewer than three classes on real estate. So, the meany that I am said, "You want to put up your life savings in a deal where you don't own the land, haven't hired the contractor, have neither the tenant or the debt in place, and worry in the middle of the night that you are going broke?"

(Somebody once told me the definition of being an entrepreneur is "waking up in the middle of the night with their stomach in knots.")

I said, "A developer ties up a piece of land and essentially lies to the lender saying he's got a tenant. He lies to the tenant saying he's got the equity. He lies to the contractor and the architect saying everything's in place, and somehow it all comes together. The epitome of fake it until you make it! Is that what you want to do?" (Note the source activities that need to be endured.)

The student looked at me and said, "I have no idea what you're talking about."

"There was a time I wanted to be a developer," I said. "But I learned when I got in the real world that I didn't have the risk tolerance for it. I don't have the tolerance for risk developers take."

That's when I realized most students, even professionals, have no framework for how to identify how, or even where, they fit in the commercial real estate industry. I started to say, "Look, here's the world, according to Jack," and the four-step framework was born.

[Note to the reader: A student in college entering the real

world has no way to correctly define their current reality in terms of a baseline for entering the commercial real estate community. This framework could be helpful as a starting point for describing one's intended future or current reality or both.]

For those of you who want to get into commercial real estate because it can produce lucrative careers, you will need to dig a little deeper. You'll need a filtering system. Since the industry is vast with varying economic factors, roles, and possibilities for your career, I've developed the following filtering exercise to provide some guidance.

Step 1: Do You Want Your Life to Revolve Around Money or Space?

The first step is to determine if you'd rather have your work revolve around money or space. To help you visualize how this looks, see Figure 8. The top arrow represents the money line, which flows from the P (Provider) of money to the U (User).

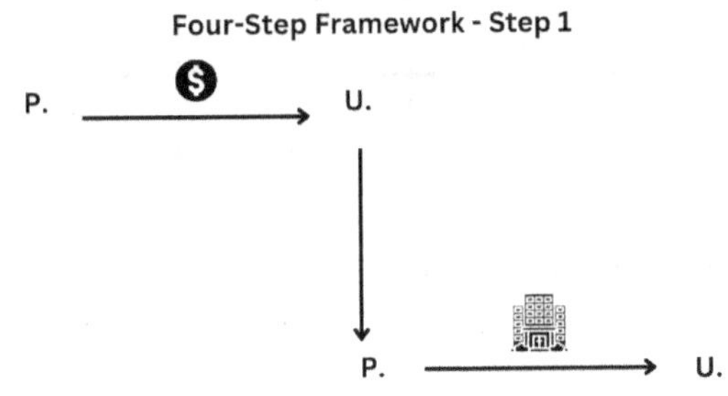

Figure 8

The vertical arrow points to the lower line, representing space, the actual physical brick and mortar.

In the world according to Jack, either you are a provider of capital to a user of capital, or a provider of space to a user of space.

Where the choices seem to intersect is that this user of capital takes the money and becomes a provider of space to a user of space. The point of the first step is that one's business either revolves around capital or brick and mortar. (And, secondarily, do you want to be a giver or taker or the money or the space?)

Step 2: Determine What Role You Want to Play

The three roles you can play in the commercial real estate industry are principal, agent, and advisor. (A tip of the hat to my brother Bruce on this one.) For me, I define each role in their tolerance for risk, where their focus should likely be, and how they get paid.

Four-Step Framework - Step 2

	Principal	Agent	Advisor
Risk	Lose $	Time	Brand
Focus	Protect Capital	The Deal	Client
Pricing	IRR	%	Fixed or Monthly Fee

Figure 9

The next step is to determine what role you'd like to play, considering the risk, focus and how you get paid.

- A principal measures success by internal rate of return (IRR). They measure success based on how they get paid, which by definition (for an IRR) is a return on and of capital. As such, their risk is losing the money owed to them. Therefore, the principal's focus will be on avoiding that loss of capital.

- An agent, typically a broker, gets paid by commission. Getting paid a percentage of the total capitalization means that the agent's risk is that the deal never closes, they don't get paid, or they lose valuable time. As such, their focus needs to be whether they are working on a financeable, salable or leasable transaction.

- An advisor's price is that they get paid by the hour or by fixed fee. Therefore, an advisor, once they have the assignment, has no risk. Right? Well, not so fast. While an advisor doesn't risk losing compensation, they do risk their image, their view of themselves, and how they want their brand to be projected. Their focus should be on the client's needs and wants, and to deliver solutions to the best of their ability, within the constraints of the brand they wish to exude.

Step 3: Define Your Desired Market

A firm's business could be local, regional, national, or international. Do you prefer suburban, urban, or rural locations? Not only should you decide the geographic footprint of your remit, you for certain want to decide where you want to live and work.

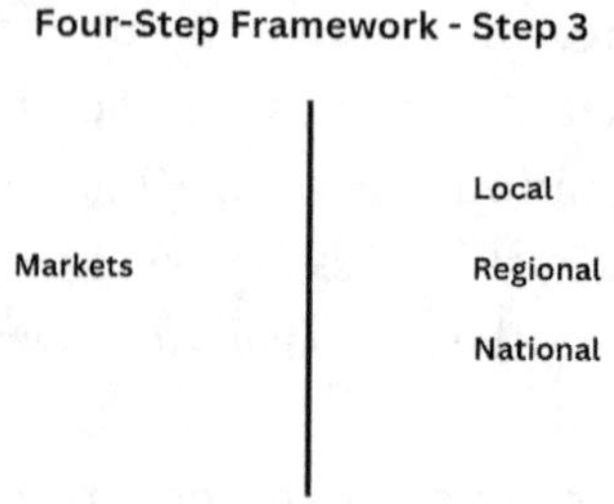

Four-Step Framework - Step 3

Markets

Local

Regional

National

Figure 10

The third step is to think about where you'd like to do business.

Step 4: Decide What Asset Class You Want to Focus On

The last step is to determine the product area you want to focus on. The commercial real estate products may include industrial, office, self-storage, retail, land, hotels, housing, assisted living, and so on. In fact, you can break this down further with sub distinctions such as unanchored or anchored retail. Anchor represents an attractive retail tenant that would draw traffic such as a department store or grocery store. How about establishing, adding to, or modifying a neighborhood? Want to build or renovate a mall? Do mixed-use properties appeal to you?

Four-Step Framework - Step 4

<table>
<tr><td rowspan="8" style="text-align:center">Products</td><td>Office</td></tr>
<tr><td>Retail</td></tr>
<tr><td>Industrial</td></tr>
<tr><td>Single Family Rental or Build to Rent</td></tr>
<tr><td>Self-Storage</td></tr>
<tr><td>Hotel</td></tr>
<tr><td>Assisted Living</td></tr>
<tr><td>etc.</td></tr>
</table>

Figure 11

The final step is to consider the kind of product that appeals to you.

I realize there's a lot more nuance to this broad-brush stroke to explain the commercial real estate industry. But it's a starting point to help understand the industry you want to enter. Either way, the next step is to do your own research. Get online and start skimming stories about people, processes, products, deals, and companies to provide more content for this contextual exercise. See if you can read about something having to do with real estate and test yourself.

Can you see whether their business represents users or providers of capital or space? Does the self-proclaimed master of the universe in the article play the role of principal, agent, or adviser? Does the firm have an international, national, regional, or local footprint? What kind of asset does it focus on? Which do you prefer?

Last, you will find it helpful to examine the list of questions coming in the next section in order for you to better assess your view of your fit for the companies you filtered through using this four-step framework. Or perhaps decide to go another direction altogether.

* * *

I have not forgotten about those of you who never envisioned entering the commercial real estate space. Regardless of who you are, what station you are in life, or what you'd like to become, it can be enlightening to take personal inventory of your skills, likes, dislikes, and know the lay of *your* land so you can guide your career.

Yet all too often, many have a singular belief that they will go to college, graduate, and have their dream job waiting for them where their income increases steadily until they can retire early and travel the world. But what happens is this: They graduate, must find a seemingly dead-end job, or hop from retail job to retail job. This is still okay, because our career paths are more of a zigzag than a straight line to success. Remember my son Wyatt?

If you really have no idea what you want to do with your professional life, I've come up with another filter, one that takes an inventory of your current self. Try answering as many questions as you can and recognize your answers may change over time. **The idea here is to deconstruct what gives you joy and fulfillment.** What skills or preferences do you think you have, agnostic to an industry or even a job. Ask yourself these questions:

- What do you *think* you want to be five, ten, or twenty years down the road?
- What *elements of your life* do you want present as you age?
- Where do you want to live? Where do you want to work (geographically)?
- What motivates you?
- What gets in your way?
- What are your pet peeves?

- What in your daily life gives you the most fulfillment?
- Are you more introverted or extroverted?
- What's your personal orientation and preferences regarding the world, economy, business, even spiritual matters?
- What talents, special skills and abilities do you have?
- How can those talents, special skills, and abilities be monetized by an employer?
- What weaknesses, gaps in education or other deficiencies do you have?
- What makes you happy? And what ticks you off? What gives you joy? (Think within the context of a work setting, if possible.)
- What have you always wanted to do, but haven't because of a valid reason or dumb excuse?
- How much money do you *need* to earn? How much do you *want* to earn?
- On a scale of 1 to 10, what level of desire do you have to accomplish that income?
- What's your risk tolerance?
- Would you rather work for, or start, a new business? Work in an entrepreneurial setting? For a major institution? Or small to midsize business?
- Do you like people, processes, or things?

After considering all these aspects, and more, can you describe your dream job or occupation? Can you see yourself doing something with a skill you enjoy performing? Can you see a business or industry paying you to exercise your skill for them in some way, shape, or manner? If this is still too perplexing, I will introduce The Donut Approach to finding what you want to do.

The Donut Approach

The area of a physical donut can be described by the content of the substance or the air that surrounds it.

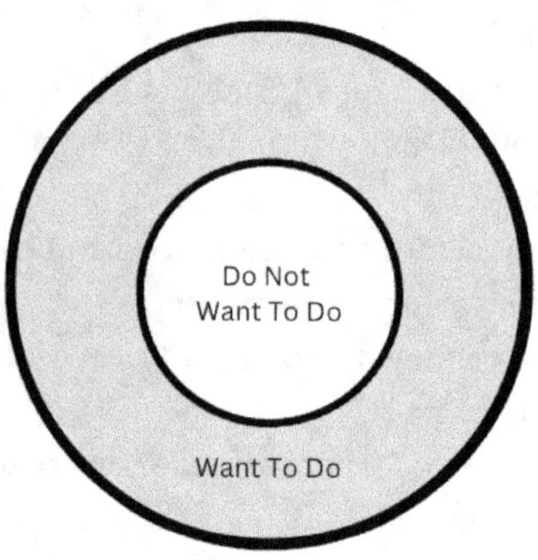

Figure 12

The Donut Approach helps you identify what you do or do not want to do.

You can ask yourself what you want to do (the meat of the donut) or you can determine what you definitely do *not* want in a job (the air surrounding the donut). Wyatt's story reflects his process for discovering what he did, and did not, want to do. You can also think of the sculptor who chips away at the material he does not want to use in order to achieve what he wants to display.

Either way, you may want to summarize your answers, form a personal mission statement, and check in on these answers every year or so to make updates. In the meantime, avoid getting discouraged with the present progress. Instead, keep the mindset that, as you grow, you will acquire skills, accumulate experiences, and develop relationships that will help you know where you want to go. I explore this further in chapter 6.

My advice is to know the lay of the land, and the lay of your land. Above all else, focus on what gives you joy and fulfillment. If you don't know, that's okay; just start with finding any job that meets your needs and go from there. The skills, experiences, and relationships will come in the process, and eventually lead you to where you want to go. It may not happen at the first, second, or even third job, but along the way, you'll gain a better understanding of yourself and find the best fit for you.

Imagine someone with artistic talents who doesn't know how this will fit into any occupation. But they are willing to learn graphic design. They find a job, or start a business, in graphic design where they can leverage their design instinct to become adept at creating PowerPoint presentations, websites, or brochures. Little did they know they entered the marketing arena, or investor relations. Maybe they can be a freelance design professional who designs book covers and does illustrations?

Through the process, they acquire a better understanding of the marketplace and what drives business. Over time, they may choose another industry and capitalize on a trend, but for now, they are happy designing beautiful things.

Quick Takes

- Finding your ideal career fit is often a zigzag path while accumulating a better understanding over time. Career management is not a linear express train to success. It's more like playing on a jungle gym in the park.
- Use the four-step framework to identify a fit within the commercial real estate industry.
- If commercial real estate is not your career or choice, take inventory of yourself and assess what gives you joy and fulfillment before you try to stick the landing.

Bringing It All Together

I am in the commercial real estate finance marketplace. I have run businesses and managed people and teams of various sizes and populated with team members of various ages and stages in their careers.

While I might have gotten into the business and industry for the wrong reasons (going to work for my dad), my career has given me joy and fulfillment. I genuinely remember the people I shared experiences with way more than the transactions I completed. It's the people, the processes, the things that I worked on that optimized our team's journey that gave me happiness. I grew, I learned, I evolved along the way. In hindsight I can honestly say I loved the journey way more than the achievements.

The catalyst for this book was a belief the young professional (ages twenty-five to thirty-five) would benefit from these career development tools. I got to thinking about the industry and how people get attracted to it, and how they find the jobs they find. Life is a journey, and the journey isn't linear. The journey is environmental; it's not experienced in a vacuum.

The context of this chapter is the framework to understand the lay of the land in the commercial real estate industry, which can be applied, in concept, to the industry of your choice. I gave you the four-step framework and encouraged you to see beyond this industry.

Lastly, experience teaches you what you do not want to do. A career formulates the meat of the donut, of what you do want to do for a living. This context of where you want to be, and a framework for how to get there, creates pull energy and freedom. However, you need a landscape, a playing field, to perform on.

4

The Power of Economic Independence

Freedom, you might conclude, takes money. On some level, you are not wrong.

If you are forced (or choose) to live paycheck to paycheck and never save or invest, then you may never experience the power of economic independence. Practically, you can never be free. As I've mentioned, my highest context is freedom (especially for careers). Freedom is being able to walk away from a job, or to start a new business, or even to take time off because there's no pressure to earn immediate income.

Bruce Wayne used his economic independence to fuel his alter ego, Batman. You may have a different career context, but I believe we share a common goal, and that is to experience the power of economic independence. How do we get there, even if we're currently unable to set aside cash for a rainy day or invest in an income-producing business? That's what I'm covering in this chapter.

I have made three great mistakes in my life. Like everyone

else, I make mistakes daily. I think the important thing to note about mistakes is that we shouldn't try to avoid them; rather, we should be quick to recognize them, learn from them, and course correct. Frankly, Barbra Streisand sang, "There are no mistakes, only lessons to be learned." I agree. We need to err to grow. That all said, I have made three doozies.

The first one was going to work for my dad. Yes, I loved the company, the business, the people, the opportunities, the industry, my career, but it was costly in terms of my relationship with my dad, siblings, and even my mom. Family businesses! For another time and story.

The second one was my first marriage. Of course, I got two amazing boys out of that union, but marriage with children that leads to divorce with children is not an easy part of the journey. That, too, is for another time and story.

The third one was investing in a business in the UK. Now that is a great story and frankly one worth sharing.

* * *

I saw Darren Shirlaw present at a conference back in 2007. The man, to this day, is the single greatest presenter I have ever witnessed. Brilliant man. He created a consulting business— the Shirlaws Group—in Australia that he then moved to London. With offices in Australia, UK, Canada, and the Netherlands, he created twenty frameworks that he and his consultants used with small businesses. Amazing stuff, really.

All four of our kids did a junior year abroad when in college; my wife and I never did. So, as my wife liked to say, we went on our "junior year abroad" in the fall of 2015 when we moved to London, and I learned the business from Darren

Shirlaw. Oh, we traveled a lot. It was fun. I met some amazing people, shared some unforgettable experiences, and traveled to inspiring countries and cities, just like we imagined each of our kids had done during a year in college abroad.

The plan was to spend six months (I stayed fourteen), learn the business, help write a business plan for expansion into the US, and either (a) move back to the states and be the country leader for the practice, (b) help hire the country leader for the practice and stay on as a consultant, or (c) leave the plan in Darren Shirlaw's hands and move on to something else.

There was just one problem, as it turned out. Darren Shirlaw committed fraud against his shareholders, which included me. And my mistake? I invested in the business before I started the job.

While his material was, and still is, clever and creative, insightful, and helpful, Darren had been, since the beginning, ripping off the shareholders by skimming money off the top and robbing Peter to pay Paul. While catching him in the act, with two other shareholders I sued Darren Shirlaw in the UK court system for fraud. While it took many years and many hundreds of thousands of pounds in legal fees, we were awarded £2,000,000. (Check out www.Darren-shirlaw.com.)

Of course, Shirlaw filed personal bankruptcy (you can't discharge an award due to fraud in bankruptcy), and we continue to chase him. He had a sad little minion in the crime, and we extracted a £400,000 settlement from her too. But we continue to chase this guy literally around the globe. But that is not the point.

The point is that I learned the expensive way about assets. Darren Shirlaw was brilliant and articulate. He made the complex appear to be quite simple and blindly obvious, and that was his greatest asset. In my experience, the smarter the teacher, the easier they make the concept seem. And one of his teachings, which I agree with, is that assets predate income.

Assets Predate Income

To have income, you first need assets to generate that income. And my thesis, the twist on his framework, is that the **number one asset anyone owns is themselves and their resulting earning power.** Let me repeat myself: There is no more valuable asset for you to invest in, to grow and prosper from, than in you, yourself. Yup, with all your perceived blemishes, I am literally talking about you. You and your earning power.

I'll cover a few specific frameworks for creating earning power in the next chapter. But the quick answer for creating earning power is to **become more and more valuable to your employer.** How do you do that? Do the work well. Learn how to make yourself more valuable to an employer. How? Acquire skills, accumulate experiences, develop relationships, and get stuff done.

How do you make more money? How do you become more valuable to someone else? As Gadi Kaufman taught me almost thirty years ago, "Folks do business with you for one of three reasons. You are (1) better, (2) faster, (3) more effective than others (at supporting them and their strategic initiatives)."

The more skills you have directly relates to having more opportunity to gain experience. More experience likely will allow you to develop more skills and relationships that you can learn from and network with. And on and on. Ultimately, as you become more valuable, income will follow.

The Valuation of Our Self-Worth (Analogous to Our Net Worth)

Because the most valuable asset you have is you, how do you establish a value for you and your assets? What is your economic valuation of your self-worth (pun intended)?

I professionally do work in the real estate capital markets. When we underwrite an asset, it is largely income producing. Ultimately, we put a value on that income-producing stream of cash flow. One tool that we use is called a capitalization rate (earnings divided by asset value). I want to use this tool as a way for you to understand how to measure and increase the value of your self-worth. One day I hope your net worth will follow suit.

Everyone knows about interest rates. The rate of interest that an investment will pay becomes a topic of discussion when an investor looks for return for the risk they are taking. Simply put, if you have $100 to risk in an investment that promises 6 percent return, your anticipated return on that investment would be $6 per year.

We can also look at that scenario in reverse, and in cap rate terms, to arrive at the total value for that investment. What would someone pay for an income stream of $6 annually (let's forget about the concept of internal rate of return for now as it's not the context here)? Six dollars of income at a 6 percent capitalization rate is worth $100 ($6/.06=$100). Now, that $6 of earnings is worth $100.

I posit, metaphorically, if you make a salary of $100,000 annually, at a 6 percent cap rate, you are "worth" $1.67 million.

As you can acquire skills, accumulate experiences, develop relationships such that you can get more done for your employer that they value, they will pay you more money. Using the same capitalization rate with the new/higher salary, your self-worth increases. If you can create enough value to be paid $300,000 annually, then metaphorically, you have raised your self-worth to $5 million.

Why do I make this point? To draw your attention to your intention to create more value.

How many people think about their annual raise and bonus? Some of us get disappointed, a few of us experience delight, but all of us think about it. While I don't want to minimize the 10% raise or $50,000 bonus, I find that too many folks take economic progression like this for granted. Too many folks job hop in search of that incremental (or step) raise and/or signing bonus. I posit that is simply shortsighted.

If we hold the context of improving an asset, investing in the asset in order to increase the asset's value, we benefit from the pull energy of the attraction caused by meaningfully larger numbers. (In my example, I intended to draw your attention to the $3.33 million increase in self-worth from $1.67 million to $5 million!)

My hope is this book will help you with a tool set that you can use to raise your worth. Metaphorically and in reality.

* * *

Does money buy happiness? I'm not advocating that. Certainly, money can buy things and experiences, but happiness? To me, happiness is not the context for my intended future. I want freedom and the power of economic independence. If a job, client, or boss is not a good fit for me, having economic independence allows me to say, "Thanks but no thanks." Then, I can move on, knowing I have enough assets and savings to carry me through to my next opportunity. If I didn't have the assets or savings, then I'd never have the self-esteem and confidence to walk out on my own terms.

Therefore, I submit to you—in practical not philosophical terms—that, in the early part of your career, **the size of your self-esteem can be correlated to the size of your savings account.** (There is a cautionary comment at the end of this chapter to consider as you indeed amass wealth.)

If you had no money in your checking or savings accounts, how do you feel about yourself (besides stressed)? Conversely, if you have $5,000 in the bank, it's only natural that you would feel better about yourself, and safer. And, for a moment, you'd be less worried. It doesn't take millions of dollars to feel better about yourself and feel less at risk. Yet, the more you can set aside, combined with the more you invest in yourself, the more your self-esteem grows. In turn, this leads to possessing more freedom, more options, and confidence to reach for the next vine, if you will recall my analogy earlier about Tarzan swinging from vine to vine.

If a lack of savings, or financial cushion, exists, then we begin to think we're not worthy or capable. We become stuck. This is why I link savings to self-esteem. It doesn't drive self-esteem, but it definitely has an impact on it. Maybe it's better said that a *lack* of savings can *erode* one's self-esteem.

Financial planners famously say that it is wise to have at least six months of income set aside so that if, God forbid, you lose your job or a big client, you will have the financial cushion until finding your next job or client. However, if you don't have that cushion and you lose that work, then the subsequent financial crisis is extremely difficult to overcome as your self-esteem takes a hard hit.

Even if you keep your job and are unable (or unwilling) to save money, your life is then dependent on your employer. Your self-esteem wavers with every threat to your employment status. If you are unhappy at your job, you must endure the pain and suffering because there's no money to fall back on. With no economic cushion that frees you to look for another job, your self-esteem is directly linked to your employment, which has made you unhappy. This is not a vicious cycle to be trapped in.

The answer to building your savings account and related self-esteem is not to merely ask for a raise. The answer is to invest in your greatest asset—you—to become more valuable and deserving of a raise. But you must also learn to save a certain percentage of money earned. This requires a bit of modesty with living expenses, but, in return, your self-esteem will increase. The greater your self-esteem, the more confidence you will have, which is necessary to achieve economic independence.

* * *

Many college graduates do not understand that when they take their first job, they are a cost and a burden to a company. When I hire a college grad, or even someone in their later twenties, I tell them, "We have a two-year game to play together. Your job is to do everything you can to get out of me whatever I have to give. And guess what? I'm going to do the same to you. And trust me, when I tell you, we're both going to feel good about it. I'm going to benefit, and you're going to benefit."

Mutual exploitation may not sound politically correct, but when called out overtly and discussed, it helps establish the context of our relationship. I'd rather encourage a young professional to learn everything they can while working for me than merely passively earning a paycheck. If they crystallize the experience and knowledge and even apply 50 percent of what they can learn from me, they will increase the value of their personal asset (themselves) and become more valuable to me and *to their next employer*.

Unfortunately, for some young professionals, they are often more concerned with how much they make in their first year. I'm more concerned about what they make five, ten, or even twenty years from now.

For the first twenty-five years of life, if you are investing in yourself to get better, faster, more effective, and more efficient, then your first job is a stepping-stone to something greater. When you do these things, eventually somebody will pay you more, and the more you can save, the more you can invest, and the more freedom you can have. Obviously, the by-product is that your self-esteem increases.

Eventually, we all need enough savings and income-producing assets to replace having to clock-in and clock-out. To retire, we need to have gained enough self-esteem early on in our career, and savings throughout our career. A fail-safe retirement strategy is more about investing in yourself now as a way to think about creating wealth in the future. I posit by investing in yourself now you are building the foundation to create wealth for your future self.

The power of economic independence starts with believing in yourself as you create self-esteem. Professionally, self-esteem might start with savings. If you don't have income or savings, then start by investing in yourself. I do that by becoming more valuable to the person who will pay me for the job I do for them. How do I do that? I cross-train. I develop skills, accumulate experiences, and nurture relationships. That's how we monetize self-esteem and increase our cap rate value. And that's what I'll cover in the next chapter.

Word of Caution

I do not want to be misinterpreted about money/wealth and self-esteem. Money and wealth can change people, for better or worse. What I do not want to convey is that a billionaire should have higher self-esteem than a millionaire. I don't even want to convey that money (as in the size of an estate such as a savings account) is the point or objective.

It's also noteworthy that I believe self-esteem is more than a savings account. It's built from a base understanding of who you are as an individual and not measured in the size of your savings. However, without a solid savings account, your self-esteem may suffer because you have fewer options and less freedom. I have always believed money is the outcome of the source activities of doing a job well.

The point is that for those early in their career, economic cushion creates freedom that can create options for career choices. Being able to invest in yourself (skill wise), being able to take the right position for a reduction in pay, being able to quit and say "this is not for me" can only happen with savings.

Quick Takes

- You are worth something of economic value.
- You are the most valuable asset you will ever own. Your value can be increased by investing in you as your main asset and demonstrating your value to your employer (or

clients).

- There is a correlation between the size of your savings and your self-esteem, which provides freedom by allowing you to have options.

Bringing It All Together

Many of us think about money more than we would like. For me, I no longer have the midnight dream that I am sitting in a college final exam for a course I never managed to make it to class for. Now, I wake up worried about going broke. Seriously. Many of us seek to own assets. Some disposable, some labeled more as toys. The truth is that assets that can create income for us remain valuable to seek. My belief is that before you do, remember that the most valuable asset you will ever own is you and your earning power.

With that in mind, I encourage you to focus less on the raise or bonus you plan on spending, and more on the increase to your monetary valuation of "self-worth" that comes from investing in yourself.

5

Converting Asset Value into Earning Power

In 1962, a young underclassman named Fred Smith pursued economics at Yale University. As the story goes, he wrote a paper outlining a business model for an overnight delivery service and was handed a C grade by his instructor. After graduating, in 1970, Fred was able to purchase the controlling interest in an aircraft maintenance company, which led to a business in trading used jets. By 1971, he had acquired a handful of aircraft, and so he dusted off his economics paper and established his business idea.

By 1973, Fred's business offered service to twenty-five cities delivering small packages and documents with a fleet of fourteen Falcon 20 (DA-20) jets. He then turned his attention to integrating an air-to-ground delivery system. While Fred was smoothing out the operation, demand hadn't quite caught on to this new idea. In fact, it's reported that he had to go to great lengths to keep the company afloat. At one time, when a crucial business loan was denied, he gambled the company's last $5,000 in Las Vegas to win $27,000 to cover the company's

$24,000 fuel bill, which kept the business alive another week.

Fred's company? FedEx.

I wonder what his professor was thinking when he gave the business plan to create FedEx a grade of C? Fred Smith was anything but average.

In 2004, Fred was honored as the CEO of the Year by *Chief Executive* magazine. Then, in 2014, *Fortune* magazine ranked Fred number twenty-six among the "World's 50 Greatest Leaders."

Why do I tell this story? Fred Smith's ingenuity and risk-taking were among his greatest assets. But that didn't automatically convert into earning power. He had a dream and never gave up. Along the way to becoming one of the most successful businesses in the world, FedEx must have presented a wide range of challenges with personnel, costs, raising capital, and low demand.

Surely, he experienced resistance and demons. In the end, he created a predictable and reliable process that his customers could ultimately rely upon. He applied the shark theory (see chapter 13 for more on this) and kept moving forward, and I'm 100 percent confident he had to invest in himself along the way. He certainly began with the end in mind. Plus, he's a great example of the principles I lay out in this chapter, which can help you evolve and, in the process, convert your greatest asset into earning power.

* * *

I entered the workforce when the generation making decisions had a view that "children should be seen but not heard," and holding the belief that one must "pay your dues" and "earn your stripes" before moving up the ladder. My generation was used to doing the work, putting in the time, and delaying gratification. When I started in the construction business, it didn't matter how smart I was or what degree I had, the fact seemed to be that experience trumped everyone and everything else.

I started wondering, how do I accelerate my experience gathering?

I've been blessed with energy, so I figured that if everyone else was working forty hours per week, I could get fifteen years of experience in ten years if I worked sixty hours per week. That was my mindset, and I went into the grind mode.

Certainly, working harder and longer has merit. Many find success this way. But eventually, they plateau because there's only so much time in the day, and working endlessly leads to exhaustion. We need to learn to work smarter.

Working smarter can take many forms. Throughout the book I mention various tools that are to be used as leverage to help you accomplish more than mere willpower can achieve. That all said, there is nothing like time in the seat to gain on-the-job experience. Over time, can you add enough experiences?

Connecting the Dots

One of my college professors said something that's stuck with me all these years. He said, "Be careful with how you build out your work experience. It can be broad or deep. Would you rather have thirty years of experience or one year of experience that you repeated thirty times?"

Another way to ask this is (as my girlfriend at Stanford, Aleen, once asked me), would you rather be an inch deep and a mile wide or an inch wide and a mile deep? There's no right or wrong answer. But I pose this to you to give you context for the content coming in the next few pages. I have always been a jack-of-all-trades, master of none. I'm an inch deep and a mile wide. So how do we know if our experiences matter?

The best way to know experience matters is if we are able to learn from an experience we had last Tuesday and apply it to an unrelated and unexpected experience that might surface next Thursday. If you can *connect the dots* and recognize the patterns, you have all the intelligence to work smarter and, in turn, convert your greatest asset value (you and your ability to learn) into increasing earning power. This is the basis for the next framework.

Be Reliable and Success Will Follow

I once had a life insurance company for a lender. My contact at that company, the head of real estate, shared this wisdom with me. He said, "Jack, your clients usually want one of two things: they either want a predictable process or they want certain results."

That stuck with me. Of course, I wondered, why can't I do both? And that's where this framework started, and it's guided me and my clients over many years. The beauty of it is there's actually freedom baked into this mantra. There's room to mold the process to achieve expected outcomes. You can zigzag your way onward and upward as you refine the process.

This framework breeds one of the most valuable, and perhaps overlooked, character traits we can develop in our careers: reliability.

You may not like what I say or the way I say it, but you can always bank on it. Whether you're starting out in business, in a career, or are a chiseled entrepreneur, the more reliable you are, the more you earn respect from others and, in turn, increase your value.

Everyone has had that person or two in their past—a relative, a teacher, a coach, a neighbor—that person who made you feel as if you were the only person in their world at that moment. That feeling of interactive support, lack of judgment, advice given from a caring space, made us feel like we could be whoever we wanted to be. Being with that person, relying on their support and lack of judgment, we felt that we could accomplish anything. Become the best we were meant to be.

Imagine surrounding yourself with people that you could rely on to have your front and back and adjacent sides so that you were free to be the best you can be. It worked for you in your youth. Now, imagine having a similar dynamic professionally by creating a predictable process that delivers certain results that others can rely upon. It's human nature to value those people, those whom we rely upon to execute our strategies to support our constituencies. That's why it's one of the best ways to accelerate your career or business. Rather than demonstrating your talents or ambitions, you will be well served by being reliable and trustworthy, which is a by-product of having built a predictable process that delivers certain results.

This is the baseline for a simple, two-part paradigm-shifting framework:

There's no such thing as a nonrepeatable act, and chance favors the prepared.

I am an engineer by education and, as such, believe being systematic and process-oriented is a key to success. I started applying this mantra early in my career; however, I share an anecdote from later in my career when I was first invited to facilitate public roundtable discussions (with up to forty participants) at conferences. I had gained enough knowledge and experience to pull this off, yet I had no direct experience in this role.

While preparing for the first event, I started with surveying stakeholders in and around the conference to identify hot topics the audience would be curious to hear others talk about. Then, my assistant and I developed a process—a work stream—that we could replicate.

After our first event, we debriefed by asking three questions that would guide us from then on (and would be helpful for you to ask too). They are—

1. What worked?
2. What would we do differently?
3. What did we learn?

Soon, we had a cadence where I could do these events two or three times a year, without having to re-create the wheel. We converted our knowledge into a conference product by creating a repeatable, predictable process that delivered expected results. As we learned more from more experience, we updated the workflow. Oh, and those roundtables got better and better over time, a result of practice and experience.

Want to convert your asset value into earning power?

Know what others want and create a predictable process that delivers certain results for them that they can rely on so they can do their jobs better, faster, or more effectively.

Your Responsibility Is Your Responsibility

Another character trait that converts asset value into earning power is to take responsibility for your actions. The next time you say, or hear someone offer, an excuse that begins with "You" or "They," beware. Deflecting responsibility, blame, and denial are ahead. For example, if a deadline is missed, it's all too often due to someone else's fault, right? Maybe the technician didn't fix your computer, or you didn't get the reports from someone in accounting, or, God forbid, the alarm didn't go off or the dog ate your homework. Obviously, it wasn't your fault, right? And what follows is a huge story.

The fact is, it's easier to assign blame than to own the responsibility and admit your mistakes. Yet, owning your responsibility is, in fact, taking the high road that increases your value and earning power. Because it makes you more reliable. If people know what to expect from you, good and bad, then they are more likely to invite you to work in their orbit. This has the added benefit of creating more experiences for you to have and include in your gumball accumulator (I explain this in the next chapter).

When missing a deadline, rather than blaming technology failure or not having the necessary information, is there a possibility you didn't plan well enough? Was there other technology available to get the job done? Could you have acquired the information another way or earlier, instead of waiting until the last minute? I'm willing to wager that, nine times out of ten, the deadline could have been met regardless of the circumstances.

The difference is in the preparation, how we respond to adversity, and how resourceful we can be. How much forethought went into not only planning but executing our assignment? Did we consider force majeure, or that sometimes things just happen? Did we consider the implications for when the assignment was due, or did we neglect to consider when we would do the assignment given the need to interact with other colleagues? Did we consider float and cushion in our execution plan?

The problem with blaming others, denying responsibility, and justifying failure is we give up control, become angry, and grow resentful. We play the victim and justify feeling powerless. Plus, it breeds a toxic culture around you that can completely sabotage your success with backstabbing and gossip. There's no learning and no progress or happiness. And most importantly, we miss the opportunity to make the work stream better, faster, more reliable.

I'm told there's a concept in addiction recovery circles that "our responsibility is to keep our side of the street clean." For example, we can't blame the neighbors for allowing their trees to overgrow and drop leaves on our yard. But we can take responsibility for raking the leaves on our side of the yard, and not complain about it.

The same goes for your career or business. We must be more aware of and responsible for our own efforts, successes, and failures. This breeds accountability by improving processes and honesty. At first, it may seem embarrassing to take responsibility for a failure, but this kind of honesty speaks volumes about your trustworthiness, assertiveness, and character. The more we own our responsibility, the easier it becomes.

The earlier you learn this, the better. I don't know too many (if any) successful business professionals who blame, justify, and deny responsibility. Plus, it's easy to spot when others evade it. I know that when I come across an aspiring young professional who openly admits to failure, and is willing to investigate what happened, this is someone who is growing in maturity and has the courage to improve themselves by seeing their mistakes as lessons to learn from. As I've said earlier, failure is an opportunity to learn. And success is waiting for those who seize the opportunity.

Future vs. Present Problems

To convert asset value into earning power, we must recognize when to act and when not to. This may sound like a puzzle but think through this with me: There's a huge difference between doing everything you can now to avoid a problem in the future and recognizing a potential problem in the future and dealing with it now (possibly unnecessarily prematurely).

Most of us work hard every day to avoid problems in the future. No one needs to be reminded of this. We want to do our jobs to the best of our abilities and play our roles without mistakes or creating problems. Of course, a word of caution: This fear of making a mistake that harms us in the future can cause paralysis in our source activities because we're so preoccupied with avoiding problems that we don't take action.

This current mindset of mistake avoidance is not the same thing as taking on a problem in the future and working on it prematurely. In some, if not many, cases, it's better to let the potential problem stay out there and address it in its proper time.

This framework applies to people too. For example, you may suspect that if your teenage relative stays on their current path, they will not be able to get into college. Well, try to remember that they are a teenager. We do not know how they will turn out, because people change, grow, evolve. They may get into the college of their choice or choose another path. So why fight this fight right now?

Instead, you can do everything you can today to love them unconditionally and let the chips fall. The point is that sometimes problems we attempt to solve prematurely are better served by letting the issue incubate until either the problem goes away or you have a better skill set, capability, or capacity to address it in the right manner.

Quick Takes

- Success requires more prowess (working smarter) than willpower alone.
- Your earning power is dependent on how reliable others find you to be.
- Know what others want. Create predictable processes that lead to certain results that they can rely on to do their jobs better, faster, more effectively.
- Own your responsibility. This kind of honesty speaks volumes about your trustworthiness, assertiveness, and character. Hold yourself accountable before you hold another up to scrutiny.
- Know the difference between doing everything you can now to avoid a problem in the future and recognizing a potential problem in the future and dealing with it now.

Bringing It All Together

In the prior chapter, I led you through a metaphor to suggest investing in yourself increases the value of you as an asset. Your most valuable asset. But in life an asset is only as valuable as the price someone is willing to pay for it. In this chapter, I suggest that reliability drives value. If folks can rely on you, they will bring you into their orbit. When they do, they are also increasing your experience set in depth and breadth. If you then can have enough experience that you find yourself able to take an experience last Tuesday and apply it to an unexpected and unrelated experience next Thursday, you will possess all the intelligence you need to succeed in your career.

II

Optimize Your Greatest Asset

6

Three Keys to Success

By far the most common question I get asked is something along the lines of, "How can I get ahead in my career (or make more money)?"

Today colleges promote first-year salaries. The implication is for you to come and get a degree from us and you will earn a zillion dollars, which I believe is a crock. Typically, the strategy young professionals seem to be using to increase salary is to job hop, finding a similar role in another company. Maybe a recruiter will persuade you to stay in the market and learn how to negotiate a better salary and perks. But eventually, this strategy can lead to a plateau. There's nowhere else to hop into a higher paying job. Then, we get confused and wonder, is this all there is? Will this be my salary forever?

The answer is probably yes unless you embrace the following. I believe that there are only three things anyone must do to succeed in their career. Any career. But they must do it every single day:

1. Acquire skills.

2. Accumulate experiences.
3. Develop relationships.

* Note: Each apply directly, and indirectly, to your vocation.

If Batman, Tarzan, or even James Bond never did these three things, they'd never become the king of the jungle or achieve world-saving levels of capability.

The same is true for your career. Regardless of where you start, focus on acquiring new skills inside and outside of your sphere of expertise, accumulate experiences by exposing yourself to opportunities outside of your comfort zone (deep and broad), and develop relationships everywhere you go.

If you only learn, and become unconsciously competent in one message from this book, it's this: These three keys to success are the only things you have to do in order to become successful in any career, but you have to do it every day.

James Bond may be a fictional character, but we can learn from him. Besides Batman, I grew up being intrigued by 007. Not because of the Bond girls (I was apparently too young to notice), but because he had a wide range of direct knowledge within his spy craft. He also had tons of indirect knowledge that gave him advantages with this work. He knew culture and style, how to fight, fly, and drive cars and motorcycles. He was adept with weapons, technology, skiing, scuba diving, and much more. His skill acquisition was awe-inspiring.

Then, he had incredible experiences including world travel, being tortured (hope you never have that), and escaping from underwater to outer space scenarios. All of this made him incredibly resourceful and effective at his work. Of course, his relationships are legendary, but he also took time to learn about his targets and collaborate when necessary.

I call this cross-training.

This concept came to me when I started going to a CrossFit gym. My son Jared, an early adopter, found CrossFit after his freshman year of college way back in 2009. The training methodology is to use various exercises, equipment, and gymnastic regimens to build strength and endurance for any kind of activity. It dawned on me this type of training applies to career advancement, and to life in general, too.

When I was ten years old, I remember watching Sean Connery in *Thunderball* and desiring to have his 007 skill sets. Over the next thirty years I learned to water ski barefoot. I learned to rock climb. I learned to ride a motorcycle. Drive a boat. I got a black belt in a martial art (second degree) and started to teach kids that martial art. I learned how to fly an airplane, added certifications and licenses, eventually earning the ratings to fly a jet and an Airline Transport Pilot's license. Obviously, I needed more skills within my industry, so I earned various securities licenses and certifications.

My point? I acquired skills. I accumulated experiences, and I was developing relationships with a wide range of people.

Now, do you think that I (or James Bond) have forty-three years of experience or one year of experience that was repeated forty-three times? This is the difference between going deep (singular focus and training, experience at one job or skill, and relationships with a few) and going wide (cross-training skill sets, variety of experiences, and wide range of relationships).

To excel in life, you will need to go deep as well as bolster those skills, experiences, and relationships with a wide mind-set. The more you go wide, the more dots you can connect with your given specialty. Plus, going wide makes you more interesting and able to connect with a wider range of people.

The added benefit? I can attest that all my cross-training has had an energizing, rather than depleting, effect on me personally and professionally. Sherlock Holmes once said that a change of problem is the best rest. For me, the cross-training concept, going from one stress to another, actually became restful.

Throughout your career, I believe the three keys to success will push you out of your comfort zone while giving you a much more balanced skill set that will make you more resourceful and valuable, regardless of what career path you choose. But it takes a willingness to push your own sense of limitations. You don't really know your level of equilibrium without moving from inertia.

I also believe that people do business with people they find interesting and enjoyable to spend time with. The broader the experience set, the more interesting are the stories one has to offer.

Gumball Tube and the Accumulator

When I was a kid, I loved chewing gum (okay, I still do, but not gumballs). When the kids started to go to bar mitzvahs, where there was dancing, the dance contest winner would get a one-yard clear tube full of gumballs, with red plastic caps on both ends of the tube. Now, imagine having that same empty gumball tube and setting it up vertically against a table. For every new skill, and every new experience and new relationship, drop a colored gumball into the tube. The goal is to fill the tube with gumballs, either imaginary or if you really like gum, you can use a real one.

The Gumball Accumulator

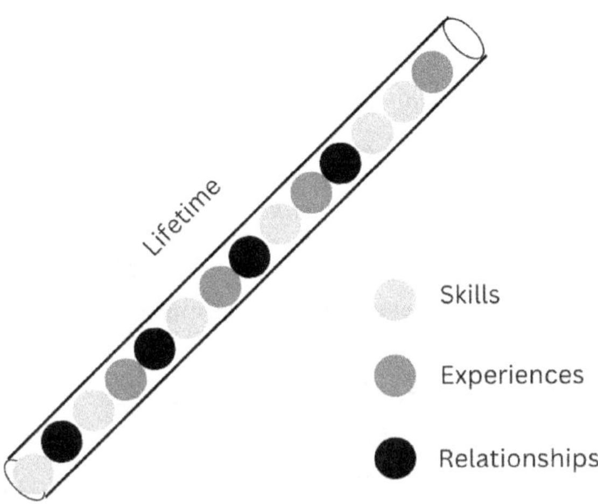

Figure 13

The gumball accumulator illustrates how skills, experiences, and relationships add breadth and depth to your career journey.

When you have accumulated enough gumballs such that the stack reaches above the table's surface, then you will be like that multicolored accumulator, filled with skills, experiences, and relationships that will help you succeed at whatever you do. As such, I encourage you, even challenge you, to add gumballs to your accumulator. Skills, experiences, relationships. Continuously. Always.

Now, not all experiences and relationships are positive. But you can still add them to your gumball accumulator. The personal transformation guru Gabriel Nossovitch once told me, "All experiences in life are neutral. The only thing that's positive or negative is the story you choose to tell yourself about that event. So, choose wisely. Make your story work for yourself." (I'll explain this further in chapter 13.)

Quick Takes

- Both direct and indirect cross-training—acquire skills, accumulate experiences, develop relationships—increase your value.
- Growth requires letting go of one vine (moving out of your comfort zone) as you reach for another.
- The more skills, experiences, and relationships you develop in any job, the more interesting and more capable you will become.

Bringing It All Together

Achieving career success and, with it, independence is simple— all you have to focus on is acquiring skills, accumulating experiences, and developing relationships. Daily. If you do, your tools grow. There is more in your utility belt to use to help you chase the next phase of your journey.

7

Time Management Tools

My brother Mike asked me recently, "I'm exhausted just listening to everything that you did last week. You've done more in one week than I have in the last month. How do you do it?"

I told him, "I started early on trying to organize myself to optimize on my perceived limited skill set. I wanted to always be able to accomplish more in a finite period of time. I learned from a young age the difference between activity and progress."

Remember, the difference is that progress is activity toward something. Then, I explained to my brother the following frameworks, which I will relay here for you.

The whole idea is that life is about making the most of our finite resources. This includes money, space, people, and time. Time management is about accomplishing the right things now and accomplishing more things in a finite period of time toward a desired outcome. And time is the most depreciating asset in life. Spend it wisely.

As with OKRs and Market Force (see chapters 11 and 9, respectively), I can give an hour-long presentation on time management and work with individuals over a period of several weeks and months before they see and feel progress. For many, developing time management skills is not easy. That said, this book isn't about time management per se. Rather it's another tool to acquire. And it's a reminder that like most things in life, time management requires discipline. **I have found that the difference between who wants something and who actually gets it is discipline.**

There are many different time management theories and tools, and they all have merit if you use them. But one thing I know for a fact is that your time management skills will change over time. What you did in high school will require a change for you to keep up in college. What you did in college will differ from your first job, which will look a lot different after a job change with twenty years of experience. The same goes for the type of role you play. A salesperson will sort the day differently than the entrepreneur starting a new business. As the demands on our time evolve, so too, should our time management tools.

Remember when we discussed the concept of beginning with the end in mind? If you know where you're going, then your activity can be progress oriented. You learn to say yes when you see an opportunity to develop your skills. If you look at my calendar you will see the priorities in my life and why I focus on them. Rarely do I consciously waste a moment. (Of course, the problem is I can't sit still and do nothing on the weekends.)

Time management is like packing your suitcase. There's only so much room (time) so I've learned to maximize the space based on my intended destination and plans. As I move into discussing the Freedom Frameworks for time management, there are a few basic questions we need to ask virtually every day: What should you pack into your suitcase? What are your priorities, and the reasons that you're focusing on them? What are the time wasters you need to eliminate to accomplish your dreams?

* * *

When I worked in my dad's office (I was around twenty-four at the time), he had a receptionist answer the phones and a secretary to screen and initiate his calls. For the rest of us, the receptionist would send us our calls directly. To me, answering those calls distracted me from making progress. I had the receptionist send my calls into voice mail. Or, prior to those days, they would scratch out a written phone message (they had phone-message pads back then) for me to return the call at a later time.

I made a plan and was executing on it. I couldn't react to every bell that rang. I didn't want someone else's poor planning or incompetent time management to become my emergency. The same goes in today's fast-paced world of emails, notifications, and messages. If we spend our days reacting every time a notification dings, we'd never reach our intended future. And that goes triple for texts and instant messaging! (Note to file: I hate Microsoft Teams.)

In those days, I noticed everyone in the office did paperwork during the day, instead of making outbound calls, visiting clients, and bringing in more business. So, between nine to five, I didn't do paperwork. I got in early, stayed late, or worked on weekends to write my submissions and offering memorandums. I began to delineate between activities happening during "public" and "private" time.

Another way to add to leverage with time management—to pack more into your suitcase—is to understand your own biorhythms. You know when you're sharpest and when your mind easily wanders. I mentioned this in an earlier chapter.

For me, I get out of bed at 5:00 a.m. and that's when, after some coffee and some exercise, my mind is at its peak performance level. After lunch, I tend to feel a lull probably because I overeat, and my system needs me to calm down. I save my most important tasks that require thought and strategy for the first thing in the morning, because that's when I am at my best. Conversely, if I need to return calls that don't take too much thought, I make those calls after lunch.

To manage these peak and lull periods, I know I must get to bed at night at a time that allows me to get enough sleep to wake up at 5:00 a.m. I know I must stop working at least two hours before going to sleep to let my brain wind down. This sleep hygiene is critical to being at my best in the morning. The point is, I know my biorhythms and do what I can to protect them so that I can perform optimally.

As you examine your priorities and think in terms of public and private modes, combined with your biorhythms, the next question is to remember the context of your current motivation. For example, in my twenties, my context was to gain more experience in fewer days on the job. Later, my context evolved into creating more value for my shareholders. Today, my context, what motivates me, is about leaving behind a legacy of goodwill by sharing with others lessons that I have learned about how to survive, prosper, and get ahead. By identifying your key context (your "Why"), you can create pull energy, and you'll be able to focus your efforts where they are needed the most.

Now, I'm not suggesting that you work twelve to sixteen hours every day. In fact, as we improve our time management skills, we should be able to accomplish more in less time. Of course, if the time allowed is the constant variable, then we can create excess capacity with those skills. Again, what outcome do you seek?

Then the question becomes, how will you fill that freshly created time block? That's when you can cross-train, recharge your batteries, look for another job, work on a relationship, read a book, take a course, or find some entertainment. Or, for those of you who simply want more, you can indeed put in twelve to sixteen hours a day and accomplish more in fewer calendar days. Freedom—you choose!

With all this context in mind, let me give you my favorite time management tools and frameworks.

Red. Black. Blue.

Some of you may remember, or still use, the famous Franklin Planner. A great tool that's stood the test of time. The overriding concept was to plan one week ahead to meet quarterly and annual goals. Then, through a system of organizing priorities and tracking calls, commitments, and messages, each day brought a new opportunity to revise your plan as necessary.

To help establish priorities, I introduce the Eisenhower Matrix, which continues to be helpful. The vertical lines of the matrix represent Urgent and Non-urgent. The horizontal lines are labeled Important and Non-important. This organizes tasks into four quadrants:

- Q1 = Urgent and important: Immediate action is required.
- Q2 = Important and non-urgent: Action taking can be done thoughtfully.
- Q3 = Urgent and non-important: Delegation or elimination.
- Q4 = Not important and non-urgent: Distractions to minimize.

Eisenhower Matrix

	Urgent	Non-Urgent
Important	**Quadrant 1** Urgent/Important **DO**	**Quadrant 2** Non-Urgent/Important **PLAN**
Not Important	**Quadrant 3** Urgent/Not Important **DELEGATE**	**Quadrant 4** Non-Urgent & Not Important **ELIMINATE**

Figure 14

Referring to the Eisenhower Matrix can help prioritize, delegate, or eliminate certain tasks.

The theory is to spend quality time on Q2. You can't live entirely in Q1 ("deal people" tend to want to). As to Q3, why bother? And Q4? Bother even less so. Life tends to draw us into Q1. However, planning—plan your work and work your plan—allows you to focus on working in Q2.

Often, I see younger professionals believing that everything is urgent and important (this is driven by inexperience), so they tend to spin at crazy rates and burn out. But I've learned that weekly planning and sorting priorities can be cumbersome, and you risk losing sight of the quarterly or annual objectives and borders/boundaries. Instead, I like to think in quarterly periods using the color code red, blue, and black.

Again, I credit Darren Shirlaw for this framework. He taught this approach to help an organization decide how best to focus its resources — human and financial. We look at quarters (every ninety days) because that's enough time to establish OKRs (explained in chapter 11) and measure performance before making adjustments in the next quarter.

The working theory is to organize your resources based on activities that are the lifeblood to the organization. The color red for the things that you just have to do. Blue represent activities that drive present benefit in your day job. Black are activities executed today that drive future benefit.

- **Red** is lifeblood. Activities you must do, but don't help the bottom line. Examples are filling out expense reports, attending some admin and team meetings, making arrangements for travel and preparing invoices.
- **Blue** is revenue-producing activities to do today. If you are not directly in a revenue-producing job, blue activities support revenue producers or the roles and tasks you were

hired to do day to day.

- **Black** are activities today that pay off in the future. This includes training, education, networking, strategic planning, and reading this book.

So every quarter, ask yourself (to put limits on your scheduling) these questions:

- What percentage of your time should be spent on admin stuff you just have to do (red)?
- What percentage of your time should be spent on your day job (blue)?
- What percentage of your time will create future benefit (black)?

Here's an example of how this concept applied to my professional life. I had a business that was making $65 million in gross revenue and about $7 million in profit. But I yearned to push it over the $100 million revenue threshold. Pop quiz: You're the chairman and managing my time. How would you like my time to be applied? Perhaps you'd say this:

- Blue: 50 percent
- Black: 25 percent
- Red: 25 percent

We decided that to drive future income to meet my goals, I needed to spend 70 percent on black, 20 percent on blue, and 10 percent on red. For the next quarter, we might shift that around, but this gave me boundaries for how best to organize my time and related energies.

Then at the end of 2007, with the onslaught of the Great Financial Crisis, the economy started to tank. Lehman Brothers failed. Several big institutions failed. My business's gross revenue went from $65 million to $5 million. We were losing money hand over fist. I couldn't shrink fast enough. Now, Mr./Ms. Chairman, how do you want me to spend my time?

We decided my focus had to be on survival. My time drastically changed to being 90 percent blue, 10 percent red (it's not realistic to think that you can bring red to zero), and 0 percent black.

Bringing these time management principles together, now you can plan your emphasis with red, blue, and black, according to the context that you hold for the quarter, sorting time for public and private tasks, and build it all into your life according to your biorhythms.

Per the 90/10/0 example, if I work fifty hours a week, then my calendar should be limited (this is the key point: time is a finite resource) to five hours of red and forty-five hours of blue activities. I can put a cap on my time management and honor my biorhythms for best effectiveness by scheduling in my calendar for the week those specific hours when I will be in black, blue, and red activities. Then, when the next quarter is ahead, I'll reevaluate how best to spend my time.

Now it's your turn. Go ahead and color coordinate your meetings and calendar to see what it looks like and decide how you might adjust your time allocations using red, blue, and black. Consider your biorhythms as you plan public versus private activities, while keeping an eye on the quadrant 2 (important but not urgent) priorities. Try it for a week, exercising discipline and border protection (see next section), being careful not to over- or under-resource the way you spend your time according to your ninety-day red, blue, and black percentages.

In the beginning, this new tool will make time management seem like a big change. But you'll be surprised at how easy and effective it becomes within a few weeks.

Due vs. Do and Border Protection

The final and critical part to optimizing your time management is to know what you need to "do," by when, in order to meet the "due" date. With this, we need to apply appropriate border protection.

Due dates set the clock ticking. Unfortunately, we all have been known to procrastinate until the night before to work on the project. This leads to risky business because many factors can go awry. Once we have a due date (#BWEIM), then we need to outline the tasks we need to do—and here's the key—in advance and *in concert with the other people we need to interface with* and make a plan.

As we work on those tasks, be aware that distractions, interruptions, and problems can take us away from these key activities. This is when we apply border protection, which allows us uninterrupted time to focus on the tasks needed to meet the deadline.

This skill set becomes important when we work in collaborative settings, because we need to account for others' lives and *their* red, blue, and black activities. We need to plan when we will do the tasks, and with whom we need to coordinate in order to meet the deadline. This is an application that begins with the end in mind.

I've seen it time and again that some people do not ascribe

to border protection. They assume they can get their job done despite interruptions and invitations. When they get near the due date, they rush and risk something going wrong. Then, they turn to you for help. If you have the time to help, that's great. But make sure it's not at the expense of missing your own deadlines; otherwise, people will keep taking advantage of you. That's where "Don't make your poor planning become my emergency" came from.

I know some of you are thinking, "My problem is my boss; what if they don't plan and are always in Q1 of the Eisenhower Matrix and drop stuff on my desk all the time?" These are attacks at your border that are harder to protect. This is when you can use the issue clearing model or other collaboration tools (from chapter 10). Ask, where does this new project fit in priority over X, Y, Z? What outcome do you seek? Can you paint me a picture of good? What will you do with my work product? Can I get it to you tomorrow or next week?

Scheduling Flexibility

When being invited to meet with someone, often the knee-jerk reaction is to decline because we're too busy. The fallacy is that we're all busy and cannot compromise with our schedule. Everyone thinks they are busy. The reality is we all have priorities and can/do make time to address them. We are also prone to procrastination, so time gets wasted on water-cooler conversations, social media scrolling, and idle chatter. If we remove these procrastinating habits, then, maybe, magically, we'll have more time in our schedule to address the unexpected surprises, good and bad.

So rather than turning down that next appointment because of being too busy, perhaps there's value in compromising your own schedules to meet. If you want to get ahead in your career, why don't you think about the experience or what you can learn from that person to get ahead?

I believe the best ideas belong to somebody else, so I steal freely. I'm not suggesting stealing somebody's work, plagiarizing, or taking credit for someone else's idea, as I've said earlier. Instead, by compromising our calendars to meet with someone, we may gain a new idea or perspective that opens our eyes to more possibilities that we then can evolve and make our own. This is also about asking good questions. This is about learning from others and, if something resonates for you, use it.

I'm not saying to compromise your calendar for every request either. We have to be mindful of what beliefs and values we operate by. We need to be good at border protection. In chapter 15, I will speak of energy liberators and consumers, but here's an example. There was a time when I found myself surrounded by folks who believed there was no personal border of another that they couldn't cross. In doing so, their aggressiveness sucked the life out of me. I had to learn how to protect those borders that effectively protected my beliefs.

I believe developing relationships is one of the keys to success. But I can't accommodate everyone all the time. I learn to compromise. I'm selective about who I meet, but I'm also open to on-the-fly meetings that may alter my schedule. Scheduling my calendar is a constant give-and-take proposition. If I give this person my time, what will be taken away? And will it be worth it? Again, your context matters.

If you're overly protective of your calendar and your project list, you're not maximizing the opportunity to build skills, accumulate experiences, and develop relationships. You're not building value in the relationship, but more importantly, your mono thinking becomes exhausting for you and others. But if you could juggle some things, then the change can energize you and perhaps take you further than you expected. One little yes can lead to a huge breakthrough. Whereas, saying no to a meeting eliminates any possibility. It comes back to learning how, and when, to compromise. And managing your calendar according to red, blue, and black.

Another personal confession: I fear missing an opportunity more than making a mistake. Yup, even old people have FOMO!

Recently, I have been wondering about the role artificial intelligence (AI) may play in my business. By coincidence, I took a call from a colleague who introduced me to an AI expert, and I took an hour out of my schedule to entertain the conversation. Since my context is cross-training, feeding my curiosities, and continued education, this black activity seemed worthy of creating flexibility in my schedule.

Then, unrelated, and out of the blue, I received an email from a woman seeking my interest in joining a board of advisers on AI at the University of Colorado. I followed my instinct and arranged a call with her, which took about thirty minutes. Although this new opportunity indeed is about becoming a program adviser, the additional benefit is I am afforded the opportunity to take a class on AI and actually get educated.

Sure, these unrelated calls were not in my plans, however, I decided to open my borders and further investigate the possibilities that may have an impact on my business in the future.

Shortly thereafter, I was invited to another zoom on AI. While I thought it was another educational session, it really was about a business trying to raise money for growth and expansion. You guessed it! I am one of their newest investors.

If I had not taken that first call (because I was too busy and needed to protect my borders), none of these possibilities would have ever materialized. It was a true sliding door moment.

Over-stressed vs. Under-recovered?

I ran a round-table discussion recently for young professionals. One of the attendees raised her hand and asked, "I'd like to talk about burnout. How do we avoid it?"

Then somebody else seconded her motion, saying, "Yes, I want to hear about work-life balance."

Then somebody else said, "I'm really concerned that my boss was mad at me because he wanted something from me on Saturday, but I was out with friends."

The discussion went on for a few more minutes before one of the attendees asked me, "Mr. Cohen, what do you think?"

"I don't think you want my answer. I'm here to facilitate," I dodged.

"No, we want to know" was the cumulative answer from the group.

"Okay, well, these are not the right questions to ask," I said.

I went on to explain. You know how when you drive down the street and then a half-mile out, you hear a railroad signal going, "ding, ding, ding." Then you see the gates going down to prevent cars from going across? Well, burnout doesn't give you that kind of warning.

What happens is you go too far and realize you're burned out. Time and self-care bring you back to normal. And the gift? The new normal will extend for how long it will take for you to burn out again. In life, business, and your career, you can move those gates any time.

Obviously, they wanted to know how to do that. I went on to explain it's a matter of these two frameworks: three keys to success and the Why. What. How. As we acquire skills, accumulate experiences, and develop relationships, I find that the fear of burnout never gets ignited. (For me and Sherlock Holmes, the change from one inducer of stress to another is rejuvenating.) Plus, if we focus on answering "why," we're going in a certain direction, then we can always tap into the motivation to keep us moving forward.

Aside from the pull energy that a solid why provides, I find avoiding burnout is as simple as maintaining a peak (stress) and trough (recovery) sine wave. In other words, we aren't over-stressed, we are under-recovered.

The first time I heard of this concept, I was reading a book written by Jim Loehr back in the 1990s. Loehr used to coach Jimmy Connors, the famous tennis professional. Connors was the original bad boy of tennis before John McEnroe. He'd yell at line judges, scream at himself, and blow off steam by whacking his tennis racket on the ground. Loehr believed that all high-stakes professionals, in sports or business, are not over-stressed. They're under-recovered. So, he encouraged Connors to blow off steam during a match because it would help alleviate the pressure building inside. Yep, the tantrums were employed as a stress reduction technique. Simply brilliant.

I think we all need to know what recovery is best for each of us. When my daughter, Lindsay, was a freshman in high school, she took breaks from high school homework by watching a particular TV show. During the NFL season, my guilty pleasure is a nine-hour Sunday spent watching all the NFL games of the day.

When I'm in New York, I enjoy taking the subway. That may seem pedestrian to some of my colleagues who use chauffeurs to drive them in black Cadillac limousines. But to me, the subway is a microcosm of virtually all my principles. There's efficiency among the chaos. There are experiences and relationships awaiting every stop. But there are other reasons I take pleasure in taking the subway.

I love the energy I feel from all the people taking the subway. It's always a mixed bag of people from different cultures with different agendas and stories. Being around people energizes me, and the subway delivers this excitement in spades.

Plus, I admit to being a bit of a control freak. I love to drive but hate to be in traffic. The only thing more problematic than traffic is being in the backseat while driven by another and stuck in traffic. The subway removes these problems, and, like clockwork, it arrives and departs to get me from here to there. It's a metaphor for optimizing my journey.

I'm also a puzzle kind of guy. I like determining my intended future and current reality and figuring out the puzzle to get to where I want to be. With the subway, the options seem endless, so I'm in charge of the best route for me that day. This dynamic goes to the points made in other chapters on understanding our biorhythms and time management. I find it rejuvenating to decide the optimal path. Should I walk to the other side of the city or jump on the subway? And where would I get off? I'm focusing on the source activity to get ahead.

Time on the subway is not lost. I use that time to prepare for what's ahead and to decompress after the end of the day. Those twenty or twenty-five minutes plus the five or ten minutes of walking to and from the subway provide me transition time, which I don't get the opportunity to enjoy when working from home. Having that transition time gives me a chance to swap my executive hat with my husband and father hat. Believe me, my wife appreciates that.

Unlike many others—and despite the noise, movements, and vast oceans of people—I find the transition on the subway allows for recovery time. I encourage you to find recovery time throughout your day, week, months, and years. The point of these vignettes is that it doesn't take much time out of your day to find recovery early and often. Factor recovery time into your life and you'll get more done and avoid burnout.

Quick Takes

- The most depreciating asset in life is time. Spend it wisely.
- What is the most important thing you can be doing now? Use Red. Blue. Black. to orient your priorities for the next 90 days.
- Know the difference between *due* and *do* and with whom you need to interact in order to get the task done. Then enforce border protection so you can progress in your own goals.
- Being flexible with your calendar can open doors, but it's not an excuse to avoid border protection either. Use judgment and be willing to flex when there's an opportunity to grow.
- Build in recovery time to minimize the effects of stress.

Bringing It All Together

Plan your work and work your plan. When you do, don't allow someone else's poor planning to become your emergency. Time management is a skill. As with most skills learned, it takes time, patience, practice, and most of all discipline to get good. Time management is a source activity, the outcome of which is time available for enjoying more experiences and more people in your life. As you fill your calendar and take on your dreams, an unintended consequence might surface for you—stress and burnout. Take comfort in knowing that you are not really over-stressed; rather, you are under-recovered. Give yourself permission to take a break.

8

Growth by Association

The Freedom Frameworks focuses on how any individual can optimize their career by seizing self-reliance and self-efficacy tools and applying skill sets that give them an edge in the marketplace. But there is one fundamental law of the universe we cannot ignore: Success is a team sport.

In this case, I'm not talking about collaborating (a skill discussed in an upcoming chapter). Instead, I'm talking about who you surround yourself with. The old idiom, "You are who you hang out with," is true. It's my principle of growth by association. I'm not suggesting ditching your close friends, but I am suggesting adding new ones. So who should you associate with?

In addition to surrounding myself with energy liberators (I explain in more depth in chapter 15), I'd rather associate with interesting people I can learn from, whom I respect and look up to, and who are more of a professional, more of what I want to become. The next question addresses where to find these people. Who are they?

The single and best accelerant to my career has been getting involved with industry associations. These industry associations, whether local, regional, national, or international, bring together the kinds of people I want to surround myself with and learn from.

When I started out, I volunteered on a membership committee for a local association so I could essentially increase my flow of interesting people that I would get to meet. While this added to the quantity of people I met, by joining the education committee, I could engage with various speakers and increase the quality of people I could rub elbows with and who literally had something to say.

There is a caveat here. To volunteer, you must be willing to serve with no overt intention of getting something in return. Do it because you like it and have the time and desire to help the platform you are volunteering for. Along the way, you can keep your agenda in mind, but if you volunteer with the wrong motivations, it can undermine your progress, goals, and reputation.

As I progressed in the mortgage business early on in my career, I identified the Mortgage Bankers Association, the Association of Industrial Real Estate Brokers, and the Illinois Chapter of the Shopping Center Council as local associations to participate in. Over time, I involved myself in the Commercial Real Estate Investor Society, Urban Land Institute, and the Commercial Real Estate Finance Council, as I continued to build my circle of colleagues.

My strategy was to serve on the education committees and become involved with picking the speakers for the upcoming conferences and workshops. Then, I'd sit in the front row and take notes, picking up helpful sound bites and anything I could learn from the experts. Over time, I selected a handful of speakers whom I deemed particularly helpful to meet with one-on-one.

One of those experts I admired was Leonard (Lee) Cotton, the founder of ARCap, an industry leader in the acquisition and management of high-yield (subordinate) commercial mortgage-backed securities.

After attending a session where he was one of the panelists, I approached Lee and said, "Hi, Lee, I'm Jack Cohen, and you don't know me, but can we get a cup of coffee?" That simple invitation opened a door for me I would have never had if I hadn't joined that association. I asked him questions, listened, and learned. Well, that coffee led to buying him breakfast at the next conference, then lunch at the next, and then eventually dinner. He became a mentor and close friend. In fact, whenever I was in Maine in the summers visiting my kids at overnight camp, I'd make a point to visit him.

Lee was older than me and had different perspectives garnered from different experiences, which I valued. Lee wasn't looking to solve problems for me. He was further along in his journey, and he could relate to some of the issues that I was having on my journey. He gave me advice and asked better questions for me to really ponder. Ultimately, I invited him to sit on the board of Cohen Financial, to help mentor me and bring the organization to heights I never imagined.

People mention networking but don't always know where to begin. I believe the real value comes when volunteering and finding mentors. For example, you could start with the membership committee in an organization, and if the group has a programming or education committee, pitch in there. You'll meet the speakers at these events, which gives you access to find quality mentors. Maybe you will get asked to join the board of directors. These conferences open access to the best people in the industry.

Let me make a distinction: Mentors lead with empathy because they've been where you are. The value of their experience can't be quantified. They can tell you, "That won't work because I've tried it three times," saving you the trouble and cost of making mistakes. Therefore, mentors improve your intelligence—by providing advanced reconnaissance—and helping you connect the dots. They pull you in the right direction as they know from experience what might lie ahead for you on your journey.

When I say mentor, do you know what I mean? Do you understand how mentors differ from coaches and consultants? My simplified distinctions are that, while helpful in a different sort of way, coaches and consultants tend to be hired to solve a particular problem. They guide and implement based on their expertise. They push you where needed. Coaches can help you ask the right questions; consultants generally give you the answers that you need.

Certain occasions call for paid coaching and consulting. But mentors play the long game with you and generally find compensation in the form of altruistic rewards.

I'm a bit of a blend, calling myself a mentor capitalist. I'm not always paid an hourly fee. Instead, I like finding entrepreneurs whom I can invest in, buying an equity stake in the platform and reaping both financial and altruistic rewards from the growth of the business from the mentoring I provide. Further, I make myself available for young professionals seeking career advice. That has led to my need to write this book. That's because I'd rather play the long game.

Playing the Long Game

When we associate with people who lift us higher, it's human nature to think short term, such as closing a deal, getting a new job, winning a relationship hurdle. While there's nothing wrong with those achievements, I prefer to live under the principle of playing the long game with my career. Borrowing this concept from author Simon Sinek who wrote *The Infinite Game*, regardless of the circumstance I'm in, I see my career with an indefinite end and infinite possibilities. So rather than focusing on closing a deal, my mindset is about creating an opportunity for relationship expansion.

A finite mindset may accomplish short-term objectives, but they can also undercut long-term possibilities. This is a concept pulled from Carol Dweck's book *Mindset: The New Psychology of Success*, on *fixed and growth mindsets*.

For example, my father was and two brothers are both outstanding negotiators (just ask them). I'd watch from a distance and learn from their techniques. What I saw were tactics designed to get the most from the other player in the deal with the least amount of give from their side. Sounds plausible, right? However, I figured that if I left some money on the table, I'd have a greater chance of winning the other player's business again someday. This long-term mindset may have cost me a little in the short term, but I believe that I ultimately won more business over time.

* * *

Growth by association is so powerful, you just never know how, or when, it will impact your life or career. Another group I love to participate with is the Young Presidents' Organization

(YPO), which was founded by Ray Hickok in 1950. At the age of twenty-seven, he inherited his family's 300-employee company in New York, so he decided to assemble other young presidents as a peer network who met regularly, so they could learn from each other to become better leaders. The organization was based on the simple context "Better Presidents Through Education." These young men and women inspire me, and, in turn, I love to participate. I have hosted round tables, started and moderated forums, given talks, and taken phone calls from its members.

However, YPO is not an industry association that's open to anyone to join or get involved and volunteer. Instead, YPO requires qualifications for membership to be met, which grants access to various forums and events. Potential membership is tied to being a president of an organization, by the age of forty, with the size of the qualifying company in terms of revenue and number of bodies in the organization. I'd compare YPO with CEO forums like Vistage, The CEO Forum, Chief Executives Organization, CEO Connection, and many others.

My point? Widely open, as well as moderately closed, associations have value to join. The opportunity to be exposed to, and learn from and with, others who share the burdens of leadership is a career education accelerant. These groups offer great opportunities to invest in your most valuable asset.

* * *

Recently, I received an email with a video link sharing about the Air Care Alliance, a nonprofit organization that helps supply pilots and aircraft for various humane needs like emergency relief. It started after a pilot from New England helped a six-year-old girl with cancer avoid an eight-hour drive to and from the hospital for frequent visits. So, I thought, "Well, I have a plane and pilot's license. Let's see where this goes."

I completed the application, took the orientation class, and signed up to volunteer. I wasn't sure if I'd be doing medical-aid trips, moving supplies, or rescuing dogs. But I knew that I would be flying anyway, and someone else benefits too.

While I'd yet to complete a mission with Air Care Alliance, I received a call from the local YPO chapter asking if I would help a guest speaker get from Jackson Hole, Wyoming, to their local event and back. Since I'd made up my mind that I wanted to volunteer my time as a pilot, my plane, and related jet fuel costs, I was willing. On a Saturday morning after she gave a thrilling full-day training on negotiation, I flew the speaker from Aspen to her home in Jackson Hole. I got to fly and made a new friend.

Did I get anything, except to share a nice dinner at the event? Who knows? Through this association and playing the long game, maybe she'll remember me down the road, or perhaps I'll bring her in on a project. Or maybe another YPO member will want a flight and reciprocate somehow, someday. I'm not sure if, when, or how this new relationship will play out in my life or career. But if I didn't raise my hand to volunteer, the long-game opportunity would have been lost.

Connect Within Your Community

It's probably human nature, but the fact is people do business with people they find interesting. Many people wall off their personal life from work life. Yet, finding connections through personal or professional ties can help form mutually beneficial relationships. What makes people interesting? Where can you find commonality among others?

If we're looking, we can find connections everywhere and, in particular, through a local community organization, nonprofit, or other worthy causes. As we get involved in organizations because of a mutual passion, and in a cause that serves a greater purpose than our own agendas, then opportunities to meet like-minded individuals are inevitable. If we serve these organizations with the right motivation—that is to contribute, and not necessarily to get something in return—then amazing connections can occur. Besides, you never know who you'll meet and who has surprising access to others through six degrees of separation.

Remember the four-step framework I introduced? The third step is essentially around your desired market location. Are you local, regional, national, or global? I decided Cohen Financial could help more people and serve my investors through a nationwide plan. While my dad dominated Chicago, I was suffocating in every meeting I went to because I had a broader vision than to dominate Chicago as Buddy Cohen's son.

Neither is bad, just different. My dad would support local organizations, where I wanted to become active in regional and national industry groups. Through my affiliations, I gained direct access to people I wanted and needed to grow the business. But I also saw how my dad's contributions to the local temple and schools connected him to our community.

Many professionals find connections through their local country club, golf course, church, synagogue, or favorite charities and arts groups. Perhaps there is a hybrid set of organizations that are rooted locally but reach nationally and beyond such as alumni associations. I'd argue the three greatest alumni associations for networking are Harvard, Notre Dame, and the Trojans from the University of Southern California.

I discovered the power of alumni associations when I was opening offices in different parts of the country. In Atlanta, the primary alumni groups were from Georgia or Georgia Tech. For Los Angeles, it was USC or UCLA. In Seattle, it was Washington or Washington State. In Portland, it was Oregon or Oregon State. In Florida, it was Miami, Florida, or Florida State. Each of these alumni groups brought touch points for networking.

You can find community within worthy causes like animal rescue, feeding the hungry, and many other amazing organizations. The most important consideration is to find something that allows you to be yourself and aligns with your personal values and passions. The best fit comes when you can do what comes naturally. Then you will have a wonderful experience that may lead to career growth opportunities. It's the Be. Do. Have. principle and essentially the theme for this entire book. Be yourself. Do what you're best at or most interested in. Have fun living your professional and personal journey. I am confident that whatever happens, you will, indeed as a by-product of you being you, advance in your career.

Over time, and based on your level of interest, you can join a committee and move up to a place on the board of directors, where more is asked of your involvement.

I've also spent many years, years ago, serving a group called Homes of Hope. We built homes for the homeless in places like Tijuana, Mexico. I used to participate with groups from YPO, high schoolers (something my daughter, Lindsay, wanted us to do after she went on her first Homes of Hope building trip), and many others in adjacent businesses on this service mission. It's more blessed to give than receive, and that was so true in profound ways.

Here's another example of serving with a worthy cause—make your own. After the father of my stepchildren, Lindsay and Alec, took his own life due to a mental illness, the family started a foundation serving mental health issues. Now, Lindsay and Alec operate the foundation, deciding which wonderful organizations to support economically with grants.

Still, the point is growth by association and investing in your most valuable asset while building relationships. It's not directly related to padding your wallet. It's about doing the right thing for the right reasons (as determined by you, no one else). I'm a purist, so, to me, getting involved in any organization for the purpose of building a business is disingenuous. However, if your heart is in the right place, relationships will come. With relationships comes the possibility of career independence.

It's the long game in play, and one worth playing for all the right reasons.

Look Up vs. Look Down

A final thought when it comes to growth by association: We can learn something from just about anyone. Therefore, I avoid "looking down" at anyone. I'd rather always be "looking up" at them.

I've known people who always wanted to appear as the smartest in the room. Their arrogant, superior posture is off-putting and condescending. I believe, at least subconsciously, they actually are going through the process in their heads of knocking down another person a notch or two to secure their feelings about themselves. In life and career, society tends to promote hierarchies where individuals are caught between looking down and looking up. While I recognize tension can occur between two people on differing slopes of growth, I try not to use that as an excuse to look down on them. Rather, I take that opportunity to look at them, and in my head build them up.

I would rather see the intersection between our interests as an opportunity to find a way to look up at the other person. I'd rather believe there's always something I can learn from someone, instead of believing there's nothing I can learn from them. By looking up at others, your growth by association will only look up as well.

Quick Takes

- Success is a team sport. Your growth depends on the people you associate with.
- Volunteering in industry, and worthy causes, leads to infinite possibilities.
- Find mentors who pull you up and coaches who help you push through.
- Play the long game to get ahead faster.
- Looking up at others puts you in a position to grow.

Bringing It All Together

My entire career has been filled with a series of sliding door moments. I'm stealing this term from a 1998 romantic comedy called *Sliding Doors,* which depicts two alternative paths the central character's life could take if she walks through the sliding door to catch a train.

None of us have a crystal ball. No one knows the causal nexus that comes from a prior experience, opportunity, or relationship. Yet, if we improve our time management to grow by association, we create opportunities for more sliding doors.

For example, when I returned from Europe with the Shirlaws organization, I went to my first US domestic conference in fifteen months. Walking down the hall, I bumped into Jay Rollins, CEO of JCR Capital, who would ask me for help with a growth strategy. About a year later, he asked me for help with selling the company. From these assignments, I developed a relationship with one of Jay's top executives, Rob Brown. Two years later, Rob moved on to become head of real estate at ArrowMark Partners, who asked me to help with a growth strategy. This led to meeting John Eisinger, CEO of Stronghill Capital, which led to a position serving that team. Would this cascade of events and opportunities have occurred if I didn't attend that conference and walk through that sliding door with Jay Rollins?

I can't tell you where I would otherwise be if I hadn't met Jay Rollins. Had I not volunteered for Homes of Hope. Had I not joined CREFC, The MBA, the IOPC Product Council at ULI or the YPO chapter in Aspen. No one really knows. However, by putting myself in position, I had sliding doors that may not have been available to me. What sliding doors are you walking through (or not)?

9

Relational Tools

Success is a team sport, no matter how well you develop skills and accumulate experiences. Relationships are the third leg on this stool, and having relational success will lead to your personal success. Heck, even Batman had Robin, Commissioner Gordon, even Cat Woman.

This book is for people who want to move from their comfort zone and raise their station in life. Yet, I can't tell you how many people I see who just want to come to work, send emails, check off their to-do lists, and go home. It is super important for associates at work to be interested in building relational capital. I strongly believe that you need to want to come to work seeking relationships; it is a lubricant for accelerating your career. The added benefit is that other people broaden your horizons and allow you to be more prepared for whatever happens in your industry, this country, or the economy.

If you'd like to add a few tools to your utility belt that make it less painful to have relationships, then read on. We don't know what will happen to our world, our jobs, or careers. I want to help equip you with skills so you can thrive regardless of the circumstances, and that means you're going to need to engage in developing relational skills that can add leverage to your own skill set or to your own career path.

Throughout my career, I've recognized the importance of relationships to my success. The result, built over forty-three-plus years, is a thick rolodex. (Does anyone younger than forty-years-old know what a rolodex actually is? Think CRM.) However, if you were to ask my colleagues what they like about me or what they want from me, they will say—for the most part—lots of nice things (I hope). What do they really want? They want me to introduce them to somebody. They want the power of F.O.J.—Friends of Jack.

You've probably heard the common saying that the people you hang out with will determine how far you go in life. But there's really no shortcut to getting there. Relationships are built on trust, respect, and some degree of mutual admiration. They take time, effort, and commitment.

I believe authentic relationships lead to good business and, therefore, agreements should almost be a formality—with the main agreement being to fight like hell to keep disagreement out of the courts.

* * *

My client's business is struggling with originating new loans in today's challenging commercial real estate market. Two of the executives, representing different departments, stand opposite from each other with a growing gap between them, holding firm to the belief that "this particular action is not my job." It's as if one is playing in right field and the other in center field and both are willing to allow a ball hit between them to drop into the gap.

For these two executives, they are both watching the ball drop right between them.

During a meeting among the executives who all have good intentions to find a solution to the challenging situation, my right fielder says something to the center fielder that ticks him off, sending him into a funk the rest of the week. They both shared the blame but were too busy protecting their territory to work together. So, my center fielder executive called me to complain, and after an hour of listening to his frenzied lament, I finally spoke up.

"You have two choices. You can either quit or you can go talk to him [the other executive]," I said. Sounds simple, but this guy isn't gifted at handling conflict. About a week later, they (gasp) went to lunch together. Afterward, I checked in with the center fielder. "How did it go?"

"Oh, it went great," he said.

"What did you learn?" I asked. "What would you do differently?"

He went on and on, and I really didn't have any idea what he was talking about. But progress was made, I guess.

Toward the end of the conversation, I said, "I get it. But I confess you missed the point." He looked bewildered. "My point is to think about the number of negative calories you burned by not simply having a conversation with him, only to find out he agreed with you, understood, and wanted to help."

Now will these gentlemen become best friends? No. But they will have a new respect between them, and perhaps they will find some answers to the origination issue. And it all started with an invitation to have lunch together and share an honest conversation.

Use Market Force to Understand Others

In relationships, it's always beneficial to understand how you, and others, operate most optimally. Sometimes, knowing behavioral types can be helpful. In my world, I use Market Force. Market Force is a human performance methodology that identifies behavioral styles so executives can improve their team dynamics.

In Market Force terms, I am an influence, and influences are about relationships.

(Market Force is a performance-oriented consulting company devoted to team dynamics, created by John Cundiff. It's a technology I frequently use in team building. My son Jared is a certified Market Force trainer. Check out his website https://www.equipped2evolve.com.)

As I superficially explain the Market Force framework, a word of caution: Please be careful with jumping to a conclusion about what these labels mean. Let me explain. The four primary styles are labeled control, power, influence, and authority.

There is no wrong type of Market Force. We need them all to have a successful team. (Beatles: John Lennon (C), Paul McCartney (I), George Harrison (P), Ringo Starr (A). The Championship Chicago Bulls Teams: Michael Jordan (C), Dennis Rodman (I), Scottie Pippen (P), Steve Kerr (A).)

I don't mean to give short shrift to the concepts and principles. What I am trying to convey is that the best teams are made up of people representing *each* of the four distinct Market Force identities. Furthering my point, teaming with different Market Force Type people, and recognizing and respecting those differences adds to the collective source activities and drives a better outcome. Effectively, the work should flow from control to influence to power to authority. That said, let me oversimplify the explanation and description of Market Force.

People who fit into the *control* category are the visionaries who love to strategize, think five years out, and believe their vision, their idea, is the right one. Those in the *power* category are workhorses who are all about the request for work. They think in ninety-day work plans. As such they can manage their team to get all their projects done.

The category *authority* is the exchequer. The authority is the one who ensures the execution happens consistent with the vision of the control. Finally, the *influence* category describes those, like me, who gravitate toward connecting others and ideas; we are the relationship people who crave action and take the hill. We are in the moment.

In terms of relational tools, the Market Force concepts and frameworks can help you identify what drives you, your teammates, and others so you can relate better to one another and optimize each other's skill sets as a team. Again, this is powerful training for a group of people, as my son Jared does for teams though his training.

Speaking of sons, remember Wyatt the theater major turned luxury watch representative? I learned from Wyatt that in theater improv the concept is to actually push a topic along, which helps the others on stage look better. Think about that in the context of participating on a work team. How wonderful would it be if everyone at work had theater improv training.

Think. Feel. Know. (aka Head, Heart, Gut)

People process information differently. We all think, feel, and have gut instincts, but we also differ in how much weight we put into any of these categories and in what order we indeed process through them. This brings me to my next, and one of my favorites, framework called Think. Feel. Know.

This framework I learned at the feet of Darren Shirlaw can be applied to knowing ourselves and others and guiding communication, even decision-making. This is not about intelligence or intellectual capacity. Rather it's about how we process experiences and information while understanding others' temperaments. Some process through their heads, some their hearts, and some through their gut. If we understand how we process information, that's a great start. But the sooner we can identify how others operate, the better we can connect and relate to others. Let me walk you through the nuances of Think. Feel. Know. so you can begin to see how it applies to many situations.

Think people seek data, information, facts. *Feel* people relate best to pictures, graphs, stories, and experiences. *Know* people just want the conclusion. They want to know the three summarizing bullet points and to move on.

Steve Jobs showed he was one of the greatest presenters in history when he rolled out the Apple products. Although he didn't know exactly who was in the audience (worldwide video conference before Zoom), he assumed there were three types of people watching: people who liked data (think), people who liked stories and pictures (feel), and people who just wanted him to skip to the conclusion (know).

His talks always gave a balanced smattering of slides that offered ample data, followed by pictures that generated plenty of emotion, followed by simple slides sharing only a solid conclusion, which employs the think, feel, and know principle.

Because my dad was a second-guessing micromanager, I became a high (on a scale of 1 to 100 when tested for Think. Feel. Know.) think person. I had a colleague (Deb McAneny, the head of real estate at John Hancock) who once told me that she valued my intuition greatly but wondered why I didn't? She made multi-million dollar decisions many times based on her gut. Whereas I didn't trust my gut intuition. I needed data.

Feel people are folks who want to relate. They want to interact with others, and typically are great storytellers (because they love to hear stories as well). Lastly, the know people just want the bottom line because they don't need to think or feel a certain way; they just want to know the concluding summary of key points so they can make a decision with their gut instinct.

How do you know if you or someone else is a Think, Feel, or Know person? Ask questions, and listen for the key words, *think, feel, know* or related energy words. Every person goes through their own think, feel, know process when in conversation or considering a decision. A simple "Tell me more about that" series of questions allows them to tap into their natural temperament and gives you insight into how they process.

When I meet new people, I try to pick up where they lean on this scale. Are they more of a think, feel, or know person? With every clue, I can use more precise verbiage they can relate to and appreciate. If they are a high think person, I can pull example after example highlighting many facts and other data. If they are a high feel, then I'll use more imagery and stories when I describe the situation. If they are a high know person, then I can just cut to the chase and provide the top three bullet points that summarize the issue.

One more example, I simply cannot resist.

When my kids were little, we would go out to dinner. The server would show up and ask us what we wanted to order (once we finished looking at the menu). Speaking up first, I would always ask the server, "Which do you like better, the steak or the chicken?"

"Steak," he replied.

"Which do you like better, the halibut or the salmon?"

"Salmon."

"Which do you like better the salmon or the steak?"

"Salmon."

"Okay, I will have salmon." This was me in my high think period.

My wife, Nancy, who while walking through the restaurant looking at plates already served, would inquire, "Over there, what is she having?"

"Eggplant Parmesan."

"Okay, I'll have that!" Nancy is a feel person.

Last, after everyone had ordered, the server would ask little Wyatt what he wanted for dinner. Without looking at the menu, he would say mac and cheese. His siblings would in unison cry out, "Wyatt, they don't have that here!"

It didn't matter to Wyatt, because (1) the waiter asked Wyatt what he wanted to eat; (2) Wyatt knew he wanted mac and cheese. Wyatt was a know person.

* * *

During my tenure leading Cohen Financial, there was a time

when the organization was stuck. The leadership team wasn't performing, which rippled throughout the business. I started to see we had too many thinkers on the team. With good intentions, they were preoccupied with gathering, sorting, and analyzing data before making a decision.

I decided to shut down all new discussions about strategy or new products and services until we figured out how to fix the stalemate. In the process, we created a decision-making model using think, feel, know for the leadership to apply with any new opportunity that came up.

We came to understand that our friction point in execution was that we had too many thinks and not enough knows. As such, we could never make a decision and move on. We concluded that anyone could come up with a new business idea. But they had to explain it to the feels in the group. If they felt good about the idea, the thinks could do the research and gather the data. Then we posed the idea with bullet points to the knows. They assessed and declared yes or no. Then we moved on.

The think, feel, know framework is a powerful skill that you can become unconsciously competent with. The more you use it, the easier and more effectively you can apply it to relationship building and improving your communication and even within team-oriented business operations. It's a lens I look through in virtually all settings. (And I find it's best used with Market Force when I am managing team dynamics.)

Efficiency vs. Effectiveness

You can be efficient with things; however with people you need to be effective. You can be efficient using emails, text, social media, even AI to help with collaboration. But I can't think of one of those tools helping to make building quality relationships effective. I'd even argue, today's efficiency tools are toxic to relationships.

What progress would my center fielder have made if he sent the right fielder a bunch of emails and texts and blasted him on social media? You can be efficient with things but not with people. With people you need to be effective. Nothing replaces stopping by to visit, picking up the phone to talk, or having a face-to-face conversation.

* * *

It takes self-awareness, discipline, and assertiveness—even courage—to make new connections. When teaching sales to salespeople, I often define relationships as the summation of a bunch of random incidental contacts.

We need to recognize relationships can occur with others who don't share our own beliefs, interests, and politics. It's a troubling phenomenon today perpetuated by social media, and dating apps, to believe our own relationships should be with others like us.

I'm old enough to remember the days when, in order to find a potential significant other, we met random people at a party, a bar, restaurant, or just doing life. These days, there's an app for that. One of the funniest nights I ever had was at a dinner with my wife, our son Wyatt, and our daughter, Lindsay. My kids decided to swap phones and they proceeded to write each other's profile for their dating apps. We laughed so hard and got to know our kids even better than before!

Later on in the week, I had a more serious conversation with my son. I told him about the days when finding a date meant going out or getting set up on a blind date. We didn't start with the foundation that everyone we dated should be just like us or have similar tastes or backgrounds. Somewhere along the line, we've lost the value of seeking diversity. "Opposites attract" just seems silly these days. Instead, our younger generation seeks out people who make them feel good about themselves, their beliefs, and what they think are right or wrong. That may work for dating, but you cannot approach the skill of developing professional relationships this way.

I fear our younger generations may have stunted relational skills because they grew up on tablets and smartphones, texting and social media. I grew up learning to "play nice" with others in the sandbox, so it's more natural for some of us older types. But it's not always easy. If we reach back and remember our desired intended future, we have to be ready to open the door for whoever comes into our lives, regardless of our backgrounds. It's part of my cross-training belief that we need to develop relational capital with all sorts of people, not just those who look, think, and act like we do. You can hold onto your belief systems, but you might want to avoid making them a boundary to developing relationships.

There is a theory about six degrees of separation, that says all people are six or fewer social connections away from each other. This means that any two people can be connected through a chain of acquaintances with no more than five intermediaries. The theory is based on a social experiment conducted by Yale professor and social psychologist Stanley Milgram in 1967.

With this in mind, you never know who may have connections to someone else who can help you along the journey to your intended future. I've always believed in networking, as in going to industry association events or other social gatherings to meet and greet, passing out business cards, and having your elevator speech ready when someone asks, "What do you do?"

It doesn't really matter who you meet, whether or not they are in your preference zone. It's more about developing relationships regardless of whether there is an immediate benefit to you. At least maybe you can shake hands, exchange cards, and leave on a good note, because something may come up in the future. After all, it's just another experience to put in your gumball accumulator. Plus, along the way, you learn the invaluable skill of connecting with people of all shapes, sizes, and colors.

Tensions in Rate of Growth

When it comes to relationships, particularly long-term varieties, the hardest path to navigate is the resulting tension that comes from being in a relationship with someone on a different slope of growth.

Slope Growth Tension

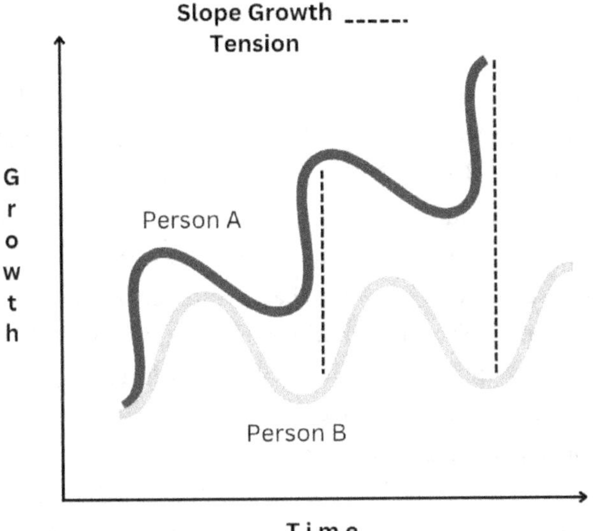

Figure 15

Tensions between two parties can increase when one is growing at
a different pace than the other.

Whether in personal or professional relationships, if one is
growing at a higher rate of change than the other, tension will
arise in one form or another. This also happens if one party is
regressing of sorts. We all peak and trough, ebb and flow, and
we do this cycling at different frequencies and amplitudes. It's
not good or bad, right or wrong, smart or dumb; rather, each
journey is unique to the traveler. As such, if the travelers are
together (think partners in life or business), stress and tension
will surface. Be mindful of this.

When two parties grow (or regress) at different rates, and different slope angles, stress is inevitable. While it can be as dramatic as clashing wills, it's more often about levels of curiosity that lead to sought-after learning that can alter perspectives and opinions.

I have always been a fan of the beloved children's book character Curious George probably because I, too, have always been curious. I am a lifelong learner, so I'm wired to ask why and how questions, and always keen to learn a new skill. However, in my first marriage, my curiosity piqued a hidden insecurity that my wife had about her failures in school growing up. I, of course, had no idea about this. All I knew was that my wife fought with me about my interests, learnings, and her perceived need to keep up. My insatiable curiosity, my capacity to adapt, to pivot, and to grow was perceived as a threat (subconsciously) by her, which created friction (and neither of us was aware of the source). Eventually, the gap in our slope growth was too great.

Doesn't this happen in business as well? Organizations don't grow linearly. I don't even think they grow hyperbolically. I think organizations and businesses grow in step variables. Companies, in a groove after a long period of time, might acquire another company, pick up or even lose a key client, or they might be sold. While we hope most organizations share similar growth patterns (x% growth per year), the reality is that corporate growth resembles more of a hop, skip, stumble, or jump.

* * *

As my brother Bruce and I grew Cohen Financial from one office producing $200 million in origination and $200 million of servicing, to $6 billion in origination and $35 billion in servicing over thirty-five years, I noticed that not everyone was willing or able to keep up with that growth.

It wasn't anyone's fault. In the beginning, it might have been about affordability. Some of the people who either we could afford to hire or who were willing to come to work for us did so with lower expectations for business progress than Bruce and I had. But as the business grew, he and I aspired to never let it outgrow us. I was able to continue to learn and adapt. For others, all of a sudden, the organization outgrew them.

This isn't about confidence. It's more about finding comfort in discomfort as well as balancing professional aspirations with personal ones. Of course, a commitment to continued education is part of this, like cross-training. But it's more about intention. At some point in all our relationships and careers, we need self-awareness to recognize we, or the organization, are growing beyond our desires, professional intentions, comfort zone, and aspirations. We must acknowledge what we want, that organizations evolve, and that our relationships with them will change—for better and for worse.

This slope growth speaks to finding your relational fit over time (and having relationship tools to clear issues out that are causing friction). If you are in a relationship, or in a business or career, that is growing and you're not willing or have the desire or the discipline to grow and keep up, I hope you feel the power of freedom (and savings) to step aside.

This can mean leaving the organization for another, or simply taking a different role in the organization that is a better fit at the time for you. Why would you want to be in a situation where the business or career outgrows you faster than you're willing to grow? Conversely, why would you want to stay in an organization that is content with its position even though you are willing to grow beyond theirs?

Three Rules for Optimal Relationship Building

It's human nature to assume the worst. I don't know why, but to build relationships on trust and respect, we have to fight the urge. Nature, and human beings, abhor a vacuum. When we don't know something, we tend to fill the gap of knowledge by making up stories and stuff, acting on assumptions, and imbuing intent. More times than not, we fill the gap with negative rather than positive thoughts.

Take this scenario for example: A coworker misses a meeting with you. Then, they don't take your call. They arrive late for the next meeting and follow that up by missing the meeting after that. It would be natural to think that coworker "doesn't like me" or "doesn't take this project seriously" or "must be going around me" to get into someone else's graces. Inevitably, we start to take this personally, get angry, and fire off an emotionally loaded email that accuses the coworker of being indifferent, too casual, and disrespectful, then laying out the consequences of another missed meeting.

This is a hole we often fall into by our own digging. Because later, the coworker explains they never received the initial meeting invitation, and they lost their phone. Then, you realize a meeting invitation was never sent so, actually, it was your fault all along. Now, you have to eat some humble pie and realize you could have avoided getting angry and hurting your own feelings.

I want to add three operational rules, or tools, to enhance

your relationships:

1. Assume best intentions.
2. Humans are human. A good person could indeed be having a bad day.
3. Ask one more question.

Assume best intentions. Do you believe that someone is consciously trying to harm you? That they woke up that morning with an expressed goal of going out of their way merely to take overt action against you? Really?

I suggest it's better to err on the side of assuming others have the best intentions in mind. Not only will this keep you from falling into your own pit, as described earlier, but it offers grace with the unknown instead of condemnation with dreamed-up suspicions. Assuming best intentions extends credit before it's spent. Plus, your feelings won't be hurt, and you won't have to send a tirade-laden email that could backfire.

Humans are human. Relationships are messy because we are human. Humans make mistakes. Humans overthink. Humans deny. Humans press "Send" before assuming best intentions. Humans make bad decisions, even with good intentions. This is one thing we can all agree on. When we accept this fact, we can be more relatable. Because a good person could simply be having a bad day, which happens to all of us.

With this rule of thumb, we can show empathy and relate on a deeper level. Relationships can be beautiful organisms that facilitate growth, love, and belonging. But if we forget that humans are human, we can miss out on what could have been a great opportunity.

Why not assume the best in others and use the default mode that humans are imperfectly human and work from there? I've sat in my share of therapy chairs and have learned that marriages often get wrinkled when we think, "If he/she really loved me, he/she wouldn't have done (or said) that." But love isn't the issue. Maybe we made an honest mistake and are willing to own it, while the other person failed to assume best intentions and recognize humans are human.

Ask one more question. What if you asked one more question, like "Did I send my coworker a meeting invite?" This entire snafu would never have happened, and you could have taken responsibility for the error. Before jumping to conclusions, I recommend taking a step back and asking one or two or three more questions to diagnose the breakdown.

You might want to ask a colleague, "Have you seen this coworker lately? Are they okay?" Or search your computer files to check, "Did I send that coworker an invite?"

The point is to think before you act, because I guarantee you will not behave in the same manner if you have the answer to even one more question.

The irony is that when we have a business decision, acquisition, or other quandary, our first inclination is to ask questions and get answers before we make a move. But with relationships, we tend to ignore this step and are willing to accept the potential negative repercussions so easily. Worse yet, the closer the relationship is, the more we ignore this step of caring inquiry.

All the points in this chapter are about having a desire, and willingness, to see relationships differently. And relationships are fundamental to growth along our career journey. We need people in our lives to help us improve ourselves and to get where we want to be. So don't become your own worst enemy. Instead, cultivate relationships with courage, be aware of differences in types of professionals as well as relational differences in slope growth, and give others the benefit of the doubt.

Care About Others

One last piece of advice: **People do not care how much you know until they know just how much you care about them.** I believe that most people can generally tell when you are faking it. If you find that you are not getting the traction you want (or believe that you deserve) with associates and clients, try to remember this pithy little axiom and put it into practice. You'll be surprised at how people's attitudes toward you will change in a favorable direction.

Quick Takes

- Be open to cultivating relationships with people, both alike and unlike yourself.
- Learn to use Market Force and Think. Feel. Know. to improve at relating to others, communicate more effectively, and improve decision-making processes. (Not to mention raise your own level of self-awareness.)
- Beware of trying to be efficient, rather than effective, with people.
- Recognize when a relationship (with your job or others) is outgrowing your current trajectory (or when you no longer want to keep up), which can create slope growth tension.

- Don't assume the worst in others. Instead, assume best intentions, accept that humans are imperfectly human, and have the courage to ask one more question.
- You will attract better relationships if you show you genuinely care.

Bringing It All Together

My favorite part about my journey is the people I have been fortunate enough to share experiences with. But I must say, sometimes people simply make me want to SCREAM. Relating to people takes time and skill. Caring, focusing on effectiveness rather than efficiency, accepting tension associated with different slopes of growth and tools like Market Force and Think. Feel. Know. make participating in and leading teams of professionals more productive.

10

Collaboration Tools

Your mother may have told you, "Many hands make for light work," and "Play nice with the other kids." Unfortunately, this is not everyone's forte or natural bent. Yet, developing collaboration skills is essential, even for the iconoclastic professional. In fact, it's more renegade to have the capacity to collaborate because most people just don't play well with others.

Life is about collaboration because the key to a successful life is how well you manage finite resources. The sooner we recognize that this is one case where one plus one equals three, the better. Therefore, having skill sets to collaborate well will add leverage to your career.

I see it virtually every day where people will be in a meeting, nod their heads and agree about everything, and then just go do what they think is right—independently.

However, if the folks in that meeting are willing, and skilled collaborators, then they would pipe up with radical candor to interact and commit to being held accountable for their part in execution on the items discussed.

The Basic Human Need: To Be Heard

Patrick Lencioni in his book *The Five Dysfunctions of a Team* asserts that results only happen if the team has a clear definition of success. Those results can only be had as, and if, all participants on the team are willing to be held accountable. They won't be willing to be held accountable unless they have overtly made a commitment. They won't make that commitment unless they have participated in a full dialogue, debate, and vetting process. They will not participate in this robust dialogue unless they feel safe. Safe enough to be vulnerable, speak their truths, and allow themselves to be heard.

A basic human need is to be heard. We owe it to our colleagues to create a safe and protected space to be heard; and for us to listen to what they have to say.

Why? Because we all have our own truths. Being willing to engage with others provides a new perspective, and being open-minded to listen to others can open your eyes as well. The converse is also true: You're not going to listen (and possibly benefit) from somebody else unless you are willing to hold the space that their truth is a viable truth.

Accept More Than One Truth

This is a concept borrowed from Eric Pfeiffer's book, *Leadership Gravitas*. While his book offers a four-step model focusing on leadership, this book helped me appreciate the fact that one must accept more than one truth. You have yours, and I have mine, just like anybody else.

Pfeiffer goes to great pains to suggest that two very hard steps need to happen prior to your accepting that another truth truly can exist: One, are you self-aware about those things that trigger you? That upset you? Anger you? And two, once aware, do you have the self-discipline to not fall for the traps that trigger you? His third step is to recognize the truths of another; his fourth step is then indeed to lead.

Although Pfeiffer's context was about leadership, valuing others' input and being self-aware has powerful applications to our collaboration context as well.

Taking his idea one step further, one trick I have found useful to accelerate collaboration (and lead, for that matter) is to find a common context to align folks.

Here's an example of poor context and the ensuing chaos: A CEO assembles the team and says, "I want you to come up with a strategic plan to grow, and I want that plan on my desk within forty-eight hours. Now, I'm gonna leave you guys to discuss the details."

What do you think the salesperson thinks when they hear "grow?" Naturally, they will want to increase the quotas and hire more salespeople, hoping to increase sales.

What do you think the marketing guru thinks? They want to increase the marketing budget so they can add more ways to reach the target audience.

What do you think the HR person thinks? They will need to hire more personnel to accommodate all the new hires in sales.

What do you think the accountant's thinking? "Oh my God, our expenses will go out of control! I need to cut back spending."

You can see how this often plays out. Each person begins arguing to justify why they need the extra money for their budget, why they are right. Because only from their perch can they know what is best for the company. They think: "The trouble with all those other colleagues is they simply aren't enough like ME!" But they are all missing the point.

Instead, they need to co-conspire, work as a team, and think about what's best for the company, not for their own departments (see Platform over Individuals in the next chapter). There is an opportunity to get the best everyone has to offer and bring it to the table for the most optimal execution. However, people need to speak up, listen, and be heard.

Frankly, in this example, this CEO didn't provide a detailed context. "Grow" is too vague. Had the CEO set a better context, such as grow by 10 percent, allowing for a 5 percent expense increase, everyone could identify their own content that contributes to the team outcome.

While collaboration indeed requires a context that participants can share ownership of, it is also about working *interdependently*. Plus, each member must accept that what is good for the platform is good for the associate—not the other way around.

* * *

When you're in a collaborative scenario, you have to recognize that other people bring something of value to the table as well, and that the project is, frankly, not about you. This requires a willingness to focus less on yourself and start thinking about how to leverage other people's skills as well. (Think Wyatt and his improv experience.) But that's not our natural state. Besides, each player in this scenario might have conflicting agendas—like wanting to earn more or to move up the ladder or to work less. Or even more likely, they bring a fear of failure to the table that only makes them dig their trenches deeper to control their situation.

I believe the world is filled with people who would rather control a decision they're ill-equipped to make than have comfort with an ability to delegate it to a subject-matter expert. It's largely a by-product of their own insecurities and their need to control and buffer their own sense of pride. They are not willing to go into the third ring—the unknown world of not knowing what they don't know. And they fear losing control, even though their control is only an illusion.

Let's start with the basic context for collaboration.

Our World

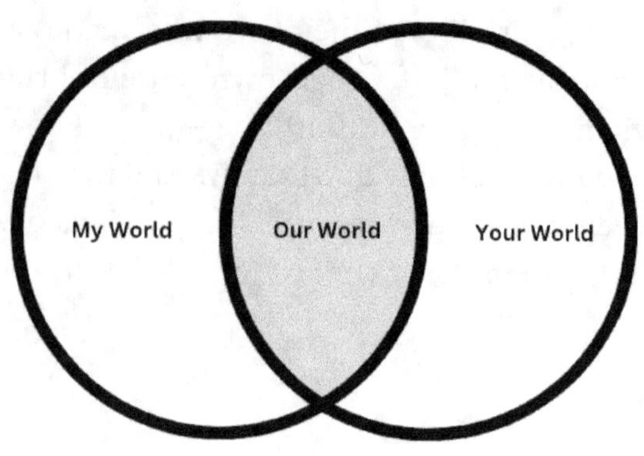

Figure 16

This simple illustration demonstrates that common ground can be found with others, which helps nurture collaborative environments.

Draw a Venn diagram, with two circles that share an intersection. One circle is your world. The other circle is my world. The intersection is our world (and where common ground, or context, can be found). This intersection reflects what we share interest in and where we can land on a common goal. We each play a role and bring our own specialties to this cross-functional team. For this team to succeed, we play by the rules such as: having the dedication to reach the outcome the team describes, owns, seeks; exhibiting loyalty to the other(s); being flexible, having determination, and learning how to overcome adversity together. It represents an opportunity to produce jointly what we could not produce on our own.

This is an example of interdependence where one plus one equals three. That's leverage. But there's more to it.

When I was asked to take over the leadership of Stronghill Capital (a small balance commercial real estate lender, head-quartered in Austin, Texas), I thought it was important to work with the existing team rather than bring in "my people." In the prior year to my arrival, the firm had closed $69 million worth of loans (average size loan of less than $500k). My context was growth as I saw a huge opportunity. That said, I needed to figure out what each of the members of my leadership were working for (personally).

Over time, in year two or three of my tenure, we set a goal to close $400 million in loans. I had brought talent to the team, but at this time had kept all those in leadership on the team. I moved people, processes, and things around and gave leadership agency to make the changes that they thought were necessary to hit our target.

While all of us rallied around summiting Mount Everest, Sandy's personal flag differed from Eric's, Art's, Robin's, and John's. I am proud to say that everyone collaborated, we scaled the peak, and each found a way to celebrate what the team accomplished together *in addition to* planting their personal flags.

Personal Flags

Someone once taught me a valuable lesson in management. His premise was that a team joined together to climb Mount Everest can work together (has to) to succeed in climbing the summit. When they do, however, each and every one of the team members essentially plants their own flag to commemorate success. As a leader, as a manager, if you can find out what motivates an individual (their personal success flag), you can find the intersection of the Venn diagram covering the team's motivation with the individual and appeal to that.

Issues Clearing Model

My most indispensable collaboration tool is the issues clearing model, which provides a method to handle conflict among individuals. No doubt, perhaps even today, we will all face a conflict with another, and in collaborative settings. Despite our best efforts to work well with others and embrace the team's OKRs (objectives and key results), there is a high probability that another person will get under your skin and say or do something that ticks you off. Then, we get worked up, imbue intent, and point fingers at the other party by assigning blame for your hurt feelings.

Or worse, we try to ignore the conflict by burying it and attempting to sweep it under the rug (possibly allowing the issue to fester).

Both these avoidance techniques can lead to a toxic exchange with another person, or with others, which makes matters worse. It's a sick feeling when there's a rub between colleagues, and many of us fall into the trap of wanting to be right instead of wanting what we want (success?). Still, there are times when people seem to cross the line, either intentionally or unintentionally, that ruffles your feathers. Or, maybe, just maybe, your issue is about you.

When I was married the first time, my wife and I did marital therapy in an attempt to save our marriage. Marital therapy led to individual therapy. I am actually a fan of therapy; however, I am also a fan of coaching. Through the years I have indeed alternated between having a coach and a therapist. This model was taught to me by my first executive coach, Delynn Copley.

The issues clearing model is for sharing your truth about the experience you are having while collaborating with this colleague. It's an extremely valuable tool, particularly for team settings. And it also works in other relationships.

Before I give you the steps, it's vitally important to address the issue as soon as possible and with a cool head or else the issue will fester, cause bitterness, and, ultimately, sabotage your relationship, even your entire career. If we can't work through issues, we'll get a reputation for not being a team player or being a bad apple. Nobody wants a bad apple to ruin the whole bushel, so this skill set is critical for the iconoclast executive.

Here's the issues clearing model you can use to resolve a conflict with another party:

- **Fact**: First, you establish the unassailable event in factual terms with the other person. (This is hard to do as it must be done without trying to disguise your opinion with an unassailable fact.)
- **Feeling**: Then, you describe how the factual event made *you* feel.
- **Judgment**: Then, you clearly explain *your* judgment about the feelings that *you* experienced.
- **Want**: Finally, you explain concisely, and without emotion, what *you* want to experience in the future when *you* interact with this person.

- **Warning:** This model is about you and the experience that you are having. It is not about attacking the other person for what you perceive that they have done to you. Nor is this about extracting an apology or, even worse, a confirmation that you are indeed right.

Between June 2022 and October 2022, three of our four children got married. As life would have it, between November 2023 and February 2024, I became a first-time, second-time, and third-time grandfather. The first and last were girls, the middle was a boy. In the Jewish religion, eight days after the birth of a boy, we have a circumcision ceremony, called a Bris. Frankly, I am not one for rituals or pomp and circumstance. However, a Bris is my favorite. Why? Because in eight short days no one can show up to the ceremony bringing any excess baggage. The event usually is held late morning, the rabbi/mohel says a few words, snip snip, baby cries, and we all have lox and bagels and corned beef.

For my grandson Jude's Bris, my wife couldn't leave her daughter and granddaughter for the Bris, and I had to go by myself. The event was beautiful. I really was unprepared for how emotionally I reacted to the service and the words Jared and Rachel shared. But I felt alone. Abandoned. And before I made it back to New York, I was really upset with my wife. While she had very valid reasons for not joining me, and she told me in advance she wouldn't make the event, I was hurt. But I needed to speak my truth:

"Nancy, the **fact** is that I went to my grandson's Bris alone. My **feeling** about that **fact** is deep sadness and I felt hurt by your absence. My **judgment** about my **feelings** I experienced was that I was abandoned on the one and only societal ritual I enjoy. It frightened me and brought back for me feelings and fears I had when the kids were teenagers about being a single parent. What I **want** is to have you by my side. I do not want to be a single grandparent."

In my marriage I am the one who wants to talk about feelings, not my wife. It was super hard for my wife to sit and listen to me clear the air. She also is not familiar with the framework either. She wanted to get defensive, she wanted to state why she was right. I wouldn't engage in right or wrong, tit for tat. I held my ground and stuck to the fact, my feelings, my judgment, and what I wanted. In the end I was proud of how I raised the issue with my wife and that this did not escalate into a conflict. I presented my issue the best way I knew how and in a manner that brought out the best of my wife's capacity to hear me.

Would you like a less emotionally charged work example?

Let's say Gretchen works for Lindsay. One day, Gretchen asks Lindsay for more paper clips. Lindsay replies with, "Why?"

Gretchen is taken aback because asking for more paper clips seems to be a simple request that doesn't require an explanation. Through gritted teeth, Gretchen explains that she checked the supply room and noticed the supply was all out, and she needs more for a special project she's working on.

Instead of agreeing to buy more paper clips, Lindsay suggests using whatever is available because expenses have been running high. Then, they depart.

Gretchen bristles with the idea of having to find another way to attach her paperwork, wasting time that could have been spent working on the project. Lindsay walks away thinking she made a perfectly sound decision, while Gretchen decides to never ask Lindsay for help ever again.

Later, Gretchen calms down and decides to use the issues clearing model with Lindsay. It could go something like this:

"Hey, Lindsay, do you have a minute to talk in private?"

"Sure," Lindsay says, as she waves Gretchen over to her office. "What's on your mind?

"Well, the **fact** is that the other day, we had a brief discussion about paper clips. When I asked you about getting more, you asked me why. That made me experience fear, frustration, and **feel** angry. It scared me. My **judgment** about these feelings was that I felt dismissed and worried about losing my job. I felt judged by you as being insignificant. What I would **want** going forward is to not feel judged but rather safe to co-conspire with you to satisfy my work needs so that we can both reach the outcome we seek for the project."

The ball is now in Lindsay's court.

With this unaggressive approach, which is about how the experience landed for Gretchen, it would be unlikely Lindsay would be defensive and justify her reaction further. Instead, Lindsay will see an opportunity to build a better alliance, so the team succeeds. After talking through this simple model, Gretchen will feel more comfortable asking for Lindsay's help, and Lindsay will appreciate Gretchen for clearing out this issue before it festers further.

I have a few pro tips here: First, be sure the "fact" is undebatable. Both parties must agree that the fact is clearly a fact and not an opinion or spun narrative. Be careful not to imbue intent or apply judgment or opinions here. Second, it would be lovely and reaffirming if the other party would mirror back the conversation to confirm they have the facts, feelings, judgment, and wants clearly understood. (My wife did not how to know to take this step in the use of the framework in my story above.) The key here, and this is hard, is mirror back means that you must use the same verbiage that was heard. There is a slippery slope that becomes toxic if the person reinterprets the message and applies their words during the mirror back process.

In this case, Lindsay would mirror back with, "Let me make sure I got this right. When I asked you why you needed paper clips, it made you feel insignificant. So, in the future you would like to not feel judged but rather safe to co-conspire with me to satisfy your work needs so that we can both reach the outcome we seek for the project. Does that sound right?"

As you can see, the issues clearing model turns down the heat and turns up the collaborative tone for both parties. The result is a better working relationship between the two, which will help the team achieve their objectives and key results (see OKRs in chapter 11).

Collaboration brings opportunities to practice conflict resolution. It's inevitable. In order to work interdependently, we have to muster the courage and skill set to effectively deal with conflicts on almost every single subject, every single day. When the emotions start heating, pull out this tool to help convey what you want the other party to better understand about your feelings and wants. Instead of pointing fingers, remember to clarify the fact, explain how it made you feel, what judgment you made about your feelings, and what you'd like to be done differently next time.

As with time management skills, Red. Blue. Black., and all the Freedom Frameworks, this takes practice. Practice indeed makes perfect.

Reality Check: Some of you might be asking yourself what if there is an unequal power dynamic? Maybe you have realized that reasoning can't always be done when somebody has power and needs others to be wrong and subservient. Remember, this framework is not about you getting your way, winning, or being right. This framework gives you agency to speak your truth and share how you experience working with another person. They may or may not evolve or change to your liking.

Paying the Price of Non-conformance

While in a relationship, at work or at home, in the spirit of collaboration, it's important that colleagues say what they are going to do and do what they say. That is a hallmark of reliability. However, when someone agrees to one thing and does another and when they do not conform to the expectations of the team, I get angry. I get angry because I (or anyone else) should not have to pay the price of someone else's non-conformance. While these words may be heavy and hard to grasp, let me give you a very easy and relatable example.

Have you ever, metaphorically, killed yourself to make a meeting on time only to find out not everyone was present, so the meeting did not start promptly? You were exhausted (and probably sweaty) from the struggle to show respect to your colleagues and be on time. You needed the meeting to start on time because you had back-to-back meetings following this one for the rest of the day. When the meeting didn't start on time, and ran over its allotted time, it set you back for the rest of your day. Why should that be allowed?

For me, when I am running a meeting, I do not allow that to happen. Why should those who comply and respectfully arrive on time pay the price of non-conformance for the person who, for whatever reason, couldn't make the meeting on time? My meetings start on time and they end on time. No exceptions.

Where is the incentive to be on time if it doesn't matter and if those on time pay the ultimate price for the non-conformance of another? I know stuff just happens. If you're late to my meeting, I am not mad. I am also not starting the meeting over or playing catch up for you. Rather, it's on you to follow up with your colleagues after the fact to figure out and catch up with what you missed. You were late. You should pay the price for being late. Not your timely colleagues.

Learn to Compromise

An adjunct to the issues clearing model to resolve conflicts is the skill of learning how and when to compromise. For those who grew up in a large family with several siblings, you know about fighting for finite resources and accepting compromise. In those families, concessions, or accommodation, must be made because there's no other choice. It goes along with the context of collaboration. When it comes to making a deal, solving a relationship, working on a collaborative team, or with career advancement, often compromises must also be made. I believe that's a good thing.

Here's why: When we learn to compromise, we learn what others need and value. We make concessions to meet their needs, supporting them, and all the while finding a way for our own needs to be met. It's creating a win-win opportunity, instead of a win-lose. Compromise is a tool to become part of the solution instead of part of the problem. It's not about rolling over and giving in to demands. Instead, play the long game so both parties can get what they need while leaving a lasting impression that could lead to future possibilities in that relationship.

Quick Takes

- Collaboration is about how to make one plus one equal three.
- Resolving conflict with the issues clearing model virtually eliminates bitterness between and among clashing colleagues.
- Learning to compromise will breed better relationships and outcomes.

Bringing It All Together

My wife and I went to overnight camp as kids. So did our siblings. As such, we sent our children away to overnight camp for seven or eight weeks. We have friends who simply do not want to be away from their children that long. Not for me to judge. What I can tell you is the amazing growth we saw in each of our children while they were away. It was the first time they had to figure things out on their own in order to get along with the other children. No mom or dad there to correct, lead, micromanage, or set up play dates.

To this day our kids' (ages thirty to thirty-four) closest friends came from summers away decades ago.

While this chapter isn't about summer camp, this is about collaboration with peers. Most people do indeed enjoy working with others on projects. They enjoy being on a team. They enjoy camaraderie. Many really don't have the skills properly tuned for collaboration. In this chapter, we learned about finding a common context, a higher purpose, compromise for the greater good, and the issues clearing model for conflict resolution.

11

When You're in Charge

So far in our journey together, all the frameworks outlined have been under the context that you are working under a supervisor or business owner. If applied, they will enhance your self-efficacy and create open doors for your career. As you increase your value, inevitably, you will be asked to lead a team or manage others.

While leadership, management and administration deserves a book of its own, I wanted to share a few of my favorite frameworks to guide you when you're in charge — and become the manager you wished you had. What follows are tactical tools when you're running the team.

Platform Over Individuals

At the heart of every successful team is the principle that what is good for the platform is good for the individual—not the other way around. The platform is the context, the content is the individual. It shouldn't be about you, the individual. However, as the platform succeeds, so do the individuals.

I like to think of the platform as an entity, a living, breathing organism, deserving its own treatment. As it grows, the team—and individuals that make up the team—will be rewarded for their efforts and contributions. The individual's ambitions must become secondary to the good of the whole. Yet, the individual's ambitions don't have to disappear either. When a team wins, each of the individuals wins too. If a football team wins the Super Bowl, even the second- and third-string players receive a championship ring because of their contributions to the team's success.

However, if an individual is unwilling, unable, or doesn't believe in the platform's best interests ahead of their own, then a fracture occurs. Imagine if everyone had disparate interests that they put ahead of the platform's. In a world where success and happiness only happen based on how well we consume finite resources, the platform at the extreme could expire from lack of nourishment. This is not the occasion for an individual's ambition to attempt to rise above the rest—at least not overtly. Instead, the individual must think, act, and behave like a teammate, contributing their best efforts so the platform succeeds.

As part of that commitment to the platform, individuals must accept another dynamic with this principle: each teammate must be willing to pay the price for others' (honest) mistakes. Because, as a team, we all are human and humans make mistakes, so long as it was in the effort of conforming to the plan.

Apply "Democraship"

Back in the 1980s, an organizational development consultant, Ichak Adizes, reminded his audience in a Young Professionals Organization (YPO) University talk that the best form of governance, where the best ideas surface, is in a democracy. Unfortunately, he said, it's not very effective with getting things done. On the other side of the spectrum is a dictatorship—a top-down approach that excels at execution but neither leaves people feeling appreciated nor comes up with the best idea nor benefits from any kind of collaboration. Adizes's solution? Run your organization as a "democraship."

Dictators dictate what to do, how to do it, and when to do it. They get fooled by their own belief that they know everything there is to know. Democracies debate and sort the best ideas, but spend more time researching, debating, and discussing than doing. The iconoclastic executive, on the other hand, recognizes their own agency to dictate—focusing on collective OKRs (objectives and key results)—but allows freedom for innovative ideas to bubble to the surface from the team.

These ideas are weighed out, and decisions are made. Consensus empowers the team to drive their own piece, and momentum begins to roll. Still, the leader must take responsibility and determine if and when changes need to be made. So, democraships blend the best of both worlds from dictatorship and democracies. It's a collaboration mindset that nurtures the best ideas while focusing the team's efforts and doesn't sacrifice getting tasks and projects done.

Why. What. How.

I have found that asking Why. What. How. can tell us a lot about a situation or opportunity. And "why" is indeed the mother of all contexts.

Author and speaker Simon Sinek, in his book *Start with Why*, says, "People don't do business with you because of what you sell or how you sell it, but why you sell it." In the book he goes on to say that the Apple brand is a perfect example. They don't sell their devices and technology entirely on what they can do or how they do it. They've built their brand on being an iconoclast—being a nonconformist. They originally wanted to appeal to people who want to be different, as well as efficient.

I want to take this one step further to include the cousins of Why: What and How. The Why. What. How. framework applies to many situations. For your career, it's critical motivation to know why you want to achieve your intended future. Looking to job hop? In addition to asking what you will be doing and how, ask why you want to make the switch. Want to build a business? Knowing why will carry you through all the what and how questions. Want better relationships? Instead of asking what or how, ask why it's important to you.

Answering why you have this job, career, or business can be an eye-opening revelation to update. Answering the why question gives you a context to use as a container to hold the content of your life. Then we can dive into answering what to do and then how to get there.

Tactically, there is more than answering why. In commercial real estate, I evaluate acquisitions and loans all the time, and I use the same Why. What. How. framework to think about and present investment opportunity. First, we need to be able to answer, "What is the deal made of?" Then, "How will we do this deal?" Finally, the rubber hits the road when asking, "Why should we do the deal?"

In a world of finite resources, why should we prioritize this investment over another? Why answers dig into the core values and motivation for making a sound decision. It is the context that gives meaning to content.

Want What You Want or Want to Be Right?

While leading a team, inevitably, team members will battle to be right, rather than for what they want—which is success.

In the 1990s, I tried to buy a business from a Southern gentleman in Atlanta. One of his partners played halfback at Georgia Tech, and the two of them had a good business originating mortgages, which would support my organization's annual growth objective. My business partner/brother Bruce and I had a plan. We had a vision and did our homework. I laid out our presentation, which I deemed to be a perfect argument for the acquisition. But we never made the deal. And the company was bought by another company not long after.

One of the last things the owner of the business said to me was, "Jack, do you want what you want, or do you want to be right?"

It took me fifteen years to figure out what he meant by that. He was willing to sell me the business, but he was not willing to listen to all the reasons why I thought I had a better business plan than he did, effectively saying that I thought I was the smartest guy in the room. In other words, did I want his business, or did I want to be right?

Translating this experience provides a valuable collaboration tool. Rather than coming to your next collaborative meeting armed to argue that you're right, be prepared to offer ways the team can accomplish the objective and be flexible enough to keep the greater good above your own personal agenda. If you do, your career will benefit in at least two ways: (1) You will have a new accomplishment to add to your quiver, and (2) you will have earned the respect of others on the team, while developing valuable relationships that may come in handy down the road.

Objectives and Key Results (OKR)

I operate with the mentality that the best original ideas belong to others, so steal freely. (Literally, I am challenging you with this book to steal these frameworks and make them your own.) I am not talking about plagiarizing or stealing someone else's ideas and selling them as your own. I am talking about learning how to leverage your career through breakthrough teachings of classic thought leaders.

Here's a great example: The venture capitalist, John Doerr, authored *Measure What Matters: How Google, Bono, and the Gates Foundation Rock the World with OKRs,* which is where I picked up this valuable collaboration tool.

That book is 300 pages long, takes me an hour to train others on it, and typically three written renditions of OKR creation before it sticks with the owner of the OKR. Then, it takes three months of updates and individual and team progress for this to begin to be an operational tool. Therefore, I do not want to give the concept short shrift, as I try to provide the essentials in the next few pages. Read Doerr's book for the full breakdown.

In a nutshell, OKRs are about getting the projects done that achieve your organization's goals. To do that, the team needs to have clearly defined objectives and key results to target. In a team setting, each individual must know what key results they need to achieve as it applies to the overall objective. As such, team members must participate in multiple tasks and projects beyond their day job that collectively achieve a team goal.

Let me simplify this with a professional football team example (which comes from Doerr's book). The head coach shares his overall objective: to win the Super Bowl this season.

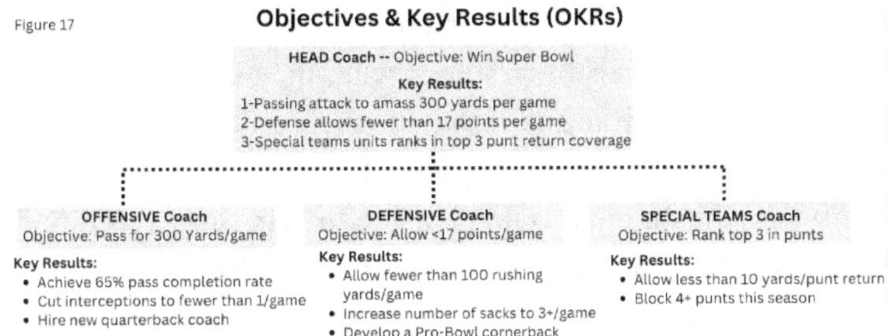

Notice the objective has a clear definition of success and a timeline. He believes it can happen only if the following key results (the KRs in OKR) happen to get them there:

1. Establish a passing attack that averages more than 300 yards per game.
2. Implement a defensive scheme that holds opponents to seventeen points or fewer per game.
3. Rank in the top three of the league in special teams play.

This gives the offensive coach, defensive coach, and special teams coaches metrics to measure their performance, which then become their objectives. To reach these key results, each coach selects their players to execute a plan that will focus their efforts to achieve their own unit's key result. From here, each player knows their role in the bigger scheme. It's a cascading effect that starts with the top and runs right down to every player on the team, even to the surrounding ecosystem that includes physical trainers, doctors, weight and conditioning coaches, and other staff.

Inherent with OKRs is built-in agency, tactical execution,

and communication flow. Each unit coach is responsible for assuring each player understands what they need to do. Each player owns their role and reports to their unit's coach on their progress—perhaps suggesting what they're seeing on the field and what adjustments could be made to help them reach their key result. The unit's coach must then report to the head coach on progress during weekly meetings. The head coach wants to know if each unit is on track, behind, or in the process of working toward their key result.

Honesty is mandatory at these meetings because the team's collective objective is on the line. If one of the units is behind, the head coach has the agency to step in and make suggestions, trade for new personnel, or make other changes.

This football team is not unlike your own organization's goals, or your personal goals for that matter. It starts with a clearly defined objective that has a measuring stick—such as grow the business by 10 percent in the next quarter, allowing for 5 percent increase in expenses. With this objective in mind, each department head can draw up a plan, assemble their personnel, and communicate the tasks and performance measures for each individual.

As a collective, each department head will negotiate how best to utilize their expenses, while the accountant monitors spending. Then, each department head will monitor their own team and report on progress to the collective leadership and CEO about being on track, behind, or in process, honestly identifying where they need help.

These OKRs require a collective interdependence, while guiding the independent tactics for each individual. When it comes to collaboration, this tool can be the guiding light that helps the team organize, strategize, communicate, and execute.

One word of caution: OKRs are not corporate goals and objectives (G+O). I am all for corporate goals and objectives as they drive the department, as well as individual goals and objectives, which ultimately drive raises and bonuses. That is not what OKRs are.

Instead, OKRs are used primarily for accomplishing projects and tasks, outside one's daily job, of three to six weeks in duration and used for teams working on projects that represent aspects of a larger project, which when combined with other concurrent larger projects being executed upon, drive department and corporate goal and objective success.

While I find corporate G+O to be around an individual's job, role, position in the organization almost in a vacuum; OKRs, on the other hand, really are about how a teammate's progress on one activity relates to, drives, interrelates with another teammate's progress on their activity. I find OKRs more like the children's song "…the ankle bone is connected to the leg bone, the leg bone is connected to hip bone…" OKRs are source activities that in the collective give the team or business the tool to get everyone's tasks done. The hidden gems in a corporate focus on OKRs and monthly updates is that OKRs can act as a collaboration communication tool.

The most important part of collaboration is communication. The teams need to be open and transparent. Hoarding information is anathema to good and effective collaboration (or team building for that matter). Nothing is more important than keeping team members in the loop.

It's noteworthy that reports say Google believes OKRs were the reason for its successful integration with YouTube after acquiring the product. They used OKRs to expand their platform, connecting YouTube with other Google products effectively, efficiently, and under budget.

Quick Takes

- What is good for the platform is good for the individual—not the other way around.
- Democraships reveal the best ideas and dictate how best to achieve an organization's goals and execute as appropriate.
- Evaluating decisions with Why. What. How. helps determine the motivation before getting into logistics.
- Use OKRs as a collaborative communication tool to guide your team and give agency to you for your own role in the project.

Bringing It All Together

Leadership is not your turn to become whimsical or capricious. Rather, my context for leadership is accomplishing more through others than on our own. When you have the opportunity to lead, manage, or administrate, the tools mentioned in this chapter are meant to help you tactically. Leadership is not about you; it's not even about source activities. Rather it's about getting the team to accomplish the outcome sought by the platform.

III

Evolve into Excellence

12

Invisible Ties That Hold Us Back

Many of you are Batman fans; some not so much. While the comics, movies, and TV shows were entertaining, if you think about it, Bruce Wayne was one sick dude. Sure, his mom and dad were murdered in front of him when he was a child. Who wouldn't be damaged by that? Clearly, damaged or not, it created some big-time demons, fears, and stories. As the character evolves, he comes to grips with being a criminal, learning how other criminals think, in order to become a vigilante. Bruce Wayne excelled in self-awareness.

I am neither a psychiatrist nor writing about why folks think, believe, and do the things they seem to want to do. However, having read, like many of you, several self-help books, I think we need to acknowledge some psychology here.

Some who apply the various Freedom Frameworks presented thus far will go further and faster than others utilizing the same tools. Why do some people excel while others continue to bump into career ceilings? The fact is, there's a fair amount of psychology and, dare I say, spirituality, which can propel, or deter, even the most ambitious executive. In this case, I'm talking about our beliefs and values.

Beliefs, Values, Thoughts

The key to this discussion is to develop self-awareness so you can identify when a belief or value is in play and be open-minded when changes are needed. Easier said than done. Why is this self-awareness hard to come by and why are these changes difficult to make? What might be holding us back? Restraining us? Tethering us to our demons?

Unfortunately, we often get pulled from our "subbasement," or subconscious, beliefs that derail us. We have beliefs that drive us unconsciously, that we seem to be overtly unaware of, that impact our mindsets and motivations. There are also other beliefs that, while not really subbasement or subconscious, are simply not at the forefront of our consciousness. This includes some of what our parents taught us, that when somebody points it out, we say, "Oh yeah, I learned that at home." Our actions come from conscious choices, even if we don't remember where we got them.

I learned from Gabriel Nossovitch, a corporate personal transformational specialist, that the strongest impulse any human being has is to prove themselves right about their belief system. I am not talking about someone who won't stop selling because their belief is so high in their product or service. Rather, I am talking about the subconscious beliefs that people have for some reason that may not be readily apparent to others, or even to themselves.

I've come across people who believe they are victims or who believe the world is out to get them. They would not, or could not, acknowledge this subconscious belief, but it's still operating in the background, affecting everyone and everything they touch (creating unwitting self-fulfilling prophecies).

$$* * *$$

Each of my four kids were diligent students in school. But Wyatt had to work extra hard. He'd start every semester really strong, and then something would derail him. While his siblings were consistently reaching close to 4.0 GPA levels, Wyatt, I believe unconsciously, started to believe he couldn't compete with them. He didn't hold the belief that he was creatively different. So, driven by his unconscious "subbasement" beliefs, he'd self-sabotage unwittingly.

By his junior year in high school, Wyatt faced what each of his siblings had faced—the college selection process. He'd observed the process, even gone on college visits with each of his siblings. He had visited his older siblings at college. He knew what was ahead. When we had our first meeting with the high school's college counselor, he was particularly petulant. I stopped the meeting.

"Excuse me one second," I told the counselor, and turned to Wyatt. "What is going on with you?"

"What do you mean?" he asked.

"I don't understand. You watched your three older siblings go through this process, yet you're behaving as if you are afraid, like it's an unknown. What's driving this?"

I hit a nerve. Immediately, he drooped his head and looked at me, as if he knew he was busted. "I'm having a hard time facing that I may not be up to it."

"What do you mean?" I asked.

"Well, I wasted high school. I wasted middle school. Even back in fifth grade, I really didn't understand what they were talking about in math. I started looking out the window and daydreaming. I kind of checked out, then I fell very far behind, and I kept avoiding it. And now I know I can't go to a college that I should have gone to."

Both the counselor and I had our minds blown with Wyatt's ability to honestly self-reflect.

"Look, I appreciate the authenticity, and the transparency. I appreciate that you felt safe to share that. Still, let me remind you that you have two years to turn this around and really do something with high school. I know you can do it. It's just that your definition of success looks different from your brothers and sister. That's okay."

And he did turn it around. That wake-up call for Wyatt brought his subconscious belief to the surface, and in the light of day, he recognized he could do something about his situation, and future.

The underlying belief system held in his subconscious unknowingly sabotaged his schoolwork and related dreams. It's like he believed he was facing a one-sided wall. But when we pass through the wall and look back, we realize there is another side. Just like if we were bound by paper handcuffs, they can be broken any time we see the cuffs are made of paper and choose to bust free. Self-awareness, or a willingness to be introspective, is the first step in breaking down the barriers that seemingly hold us back.

Therefore, as we pursue career freedom or our intended future, we have to challenge our beliefs sometimes. We may need another perspective to see the other side of the wall in front of us in order to break free from the paper handcuffs.

(A shout out to therapy and coaching. Sometimes we need an outsider and a safe space and fresh process to awaken our awareness of the beliefs that control us.)

Values Ripple Effect

If we aren't in touch with who we are at the core, we may find ourselves acting and reacting to the wrong impulses. As they say, "If you stand for nothing, you'll fall for anything." It's too easy to adopt values that are not necessarily healthy, productive, or even beneficial to your journey. They can become your new default without even recognizing it. You can be influenced by a competitor who lies, cheats, and steals. You may become like that competitor if you don't have an operating value system of your own.

Whatever your beliefs and values are, they are yours. With self-awareness and staying in touch with what moves us, we can determine where we want to go and, ultimately, how we get there.

For example, if I hold a belief that I'm a morally driven person, then a value that pulls me forward is that I define right and wrong based on the standard of excellence that I aspire to, not what I can get away with. This value helps me decide about what I believe is doing the right thing. Conversely, one could argue that beliefs come from values. Either way, our actions are driven by our thoughts, which come from our beliefs and values.

If you believe in your ability to succeed, then you will value opportunities to optimize your greatest asset. Your thoughts, in turn, will determine the actions to learn and practice the skills to get ahead. I'll give you a few frameworks for thoughts (and actions) that breed excellence in the next chapter. For now, let's dive into the deep waters of beliefs and values.

Beliefs/Values/Thoughts

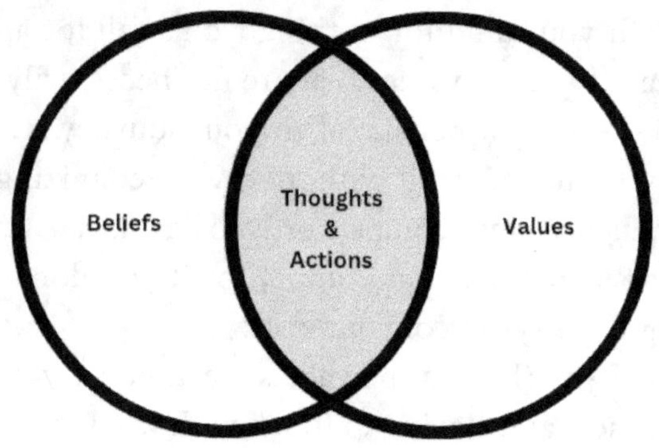

Figure 18

Thoughts (and actions) are the intersection between your beliefs and values.

A few years back, a young man we hired out of college came into my office after working with me for about forty-five days. He said, "I believe I'm doing a great job, so I think I deserve a raise."

"Really? Wow," I replied. But I wanted to say, "Huh? Are you outta your mind? Because you think you're doing a good job, you deserve a raise?" After holding my tongue, I asked, "Okay, where are you creating additional value for me?"

"Not sure, but my mother told me I should ask for a raise," he replied. "Because it never hurts to ask."

"Call your mother, put her on the phone so I can straighten this out," I said.

"No, no, don't do that," he said.

Immediately, I saw how values have a ripple effect. I knew two things: This young man needed to understand the context for his job, and he needed a content lesson in self-awareness. Nobody who knows the context for the business, and has self-awareness, would ask for a raise because their mother told them to after forty-five days on the job. Without a firm belief in himself, he was easily swayed by his mother's advice that he deserved a raise. His belief was that it doesn't hurt to ask. Or it was simply that he was brought up to do whatever his mother told him to do.

While it's not my place to judge him for his beliefs and values, he was wrong on both accounts. If, however, his belief was that his performance would do the talking, then he'd never have had to ask for a raise. Then, his values would be along the lines of increasing value to the company and increasing the value of his greatest asset: himself (a recurring theme in this book).

My dad was all about respect and would always moan and groan about wanting respect. Yet, no one treated another person more poorly or less disrespectfully than he did when he got angry and felt he had to scream at them. His lens was clouded. It was more important to him to be respected than it was to be liked. Imagine how these values rippled through the workplace.

On the other side of the coin, I have worked with the leader at ArrowMark who believes in people, values the love of others, and doesn't want to let anyone down. Now imagine how that affects his ability to have hard conversations with individuals on his team. From these two examples, we can see how a corporate culture can differ significantly by the leadership's beliefs and values. We all have beliefs and values that impact the world around us.

Loyalty Can Be a Valuable, Bi-directional Ally

Loyalty may seem to be an anti-iconoclast value. But, in fact, it's more iconoclastic to be loyal to your beliefs and values and to the people who support you, your beliefs, and values. Loyalty is a powerful ally, and yet has to be weighed constantly. I can be loyal to my beliefs and values. I can also be loyal to the person who gave me a job and the platform we all work for.

I always tell people when I hire them, "Look, I approach our work together as if we will work our entire careers together, knowing that's not likely going to happen. It may surprise you, but I hope you are looking for a job every day, because tomorrow when you show up for work, I know you want to be here."

The last thing I want is an employee who can't get a job someplace else. However, if they are looking elsewhere, I want them to come talk to me. Maybe I can help modify their role here or help them find their next job. I'm honoring my belief in freedom. Freedom for me, freedom for them, freedom to choose the journey that is right for them. I am exuding a value of loyalty to my team and to my value system.

Ideally, loyalty is bi-directional, from person to person,

person to platform, and platform to person. Wouldn't it be a wonderful world if our platforms were loyal to our people and our people were equally loyal to our platform? Am I being naive when I am unconditionally loyal to a teammate? After you read about my next story, maybe you would coach me by pointing out that in the long run loyalty works best if it goes both ways.

Once I had a young man tell me that he was leaving the firm even though we had just given him a promotion and he was now leading an entire department. He asked me to sign a release from his employment so he could start with the new company the following week. Essentially, he would be taking the people, processes, and everything he learned from our firm to go across the street to our competitor. And he wanted me to pay out his bonus.

I said, "Okay, well sure. You do your thing. I'll do my thing. But why don't you give me forty-five days notice? That way, you can get paid your bonus and I can honor your contribution to the company."

"No, I've already committed to starting to work next week," he said.

"Okay, but the bonuses are paid based on attendance at the time of year when bonuses are paid, so you'll lose that," which would have been nearly half a million dollars for this young man.

While I showed him loyalty, I invested in him and his career growth, and he ended up taking about ten of our employees and decimating that line of business. But his disloyalty, and maybe a lack of common sense, cost him a sizable bonus.

* * *

As we dig further, we will find many more beliefs and values that define who we are and who we want to be. For me, I believe in "we" instead of "me." I value teamwork, respecting others while maintaining my own self-respect. I believe in discipline and value the patience, practice, and persistence required to grow. I believe success is about inspiration *and* perspiration. I value kindness, compassion, and love. I don't believe success is a zero-sum game.

I want everyone to do well. I don't want my good fortune to be at the expense of somebody else. And to the contrary, where I can afford to help somebody else who doesn't have good fortune, I want to help. In the end, I believe that my job is to do everything I can to enhance my skill set so that my execution on behalf of others is better.

Beliefs and values are highly personal, so I'm not going to tell you how to operate. Still, by reading this book, I'm sure we share at least one belief and one value: We believe we can succeed, and our value is to always be learning and growing.

Gaming the System

While hosting my son's rehearsal dinner the night before his wedding, I struck up a conversation with my nephew, who was about twenty-five at the time and working in Los Angeles for Goldman Sachs. He mentioned that he wanted to move to New York. I asked, "I wonder if there's anything I could do to help you find a job there. What are you looking for?"

"Well, Uncle Jack, I am looking to find a place where I can make the most amount of money in the shortest amount of time for the least amount of work," he said without flinching.

I looked at him a bit bewildered. I even thought to myself, life is easy if you do the hard stuff; hard if all you do is the easy stuff. But I bit my tongue and told him that I was sorry, and that I did not think that I could help him. I simply did not know how.

There's nothing inherently wrong with my nephew's desire. But since I value grit, the journey, loyalty in the workplace, working smart and working hard for someone else's business, playing the long game, and creating value for the platform, there's nothing I could do to help him.

He wanted to grab a new vine based on a belief that New York would be better for him. His value was that he would work hard at finding a job that paid more for less effort in less time. To me, that's an example of trying to game the system, instead of playing the long game.

When somebody sits back and tries to game the system, they're assessing someone else's, or the institution's, values to find where the cracks are. Then, they position themselves to take advantage of the loophole in an effort to get ahead. This may lead to short-term advancement, but in my opinion eventually those vines run out.

But let me make the distinction that I believe working smart while working hard is not the same as gaming the system and looking for a shortcut. There are no shortcuts when playing a long game.

Although I know there are people who try to think their way to an optimal solution, my belief is Be. Do. Have., as outlined earlier. While it's not about me, and I am not telling you that you should think like me. I believe it's more rewarding to decide who you want to be, then do the work to get what you want. I value acquiring skills, accumulating experiences, and developing relationships to get ahead. Instead of sitting on the sidelines looking for ways to game the system, I'd rather be in the game and have some say in the outcome. As my friend Sam Saxton is fond of saying, "You gotta just do the work!" Grit.

Personally, I don't think jumping from one perceived happiness vine to another is the answer to a fulfilling and rewarding career. I value, and enjoy, the process of doing the work, growing as an individual, and creating a future with freedom. I value recognition, not in a narcissistic way but in a Batman way. I want others to know that if they need help, they can come to me. I want to be heard and understood because I believe what I offer can be of great assistance. You don't have to agree with me all the time, but I believe that my skills, experiences, and relationships are valuable to me and to others.

I don't believe that people leave companies for money alone. Rather, they leave because something about their situation conflicts with their beliefs and values, even if they're not aware of them. (Now, if you're constantly getting screwed economically, that's different.) Typically, an underlying current doesn't sit well, and therefore seems to necessitate a move.

If you can connect the dots, the next move will be for a leader you want to work for, a culture that fits you, and where there's opportunity to acquire skills, experiences, and relationships in a role you really love.

The Values Challenge

The challenge comes when our beliefs and values are tested. Will we honor or compromise them?

Integrity, which to me means doing the right thing even when nobody's watching, is often challenged. I share the following personal story as an example when I faced an integrity challenge. This is not to make me sound holier-than-thou, because I'm sure I've failed this test other times in my life. Still, for demonstration purposes, I had an opportunity to do what I thought was the right thing when I moved from California to Denver to take my first job.

When I arrived in Denver, I wrote a check out of my California account to my Denver account and closed the California bank account. I wrote a check for $2,600 to empty the account at the local bank. But the bank made a mistake, clearing the check through the Federal Reserve for $26, leaving me a net profit of $2,574. I had to choose between keeping the money and capitalizing on the bank's error or taking action to correct the wrong. What would you do?

I decided to call the bank and ask them to correct the error. Why? Because the conflict required me to decide what to do based on the value I hold dear. If I didn't value integrity, I would have kept the money. Besides, it just didn't feel right to me. [Note to the reader: when I called the bank, they rejected the fact that the bank made an error. I went up the corporate chain three levels to the Branch President for the bank to conclude I was not a crackpot and that they should look into it. In point of fact, the check actually cleared, through the Federal Reserve Banking system incorrectly. Their error, the error of the US Banking system, created a windfall for me that I had to fight to give back!]

The point is that our values will be challenged on ethical, moral, and legal levels. But our values make us who we are, so staying true to them honors who you are and what you stand for. Over time, these values become valuable to others, which creates more opportunities to excel in your career.

Are you aware of the beliefs running your system? Could you be struggling to make progress because of hidden beliefs that continue to undermine your success? It may be worth a systems check on a regular basis. How about the values you keep front and center in your choices? Are they helping or hurting you to move forward? By examining your beliefs and values, and staying true to them, you will make decisions that matter to you and others, and ultimately you will achieve freedom.

Quick Takes

- Operating with beliefs and values helps you stand for something—and fall for nothing.
- Beliefs and values guide every decision, impacting you and those around you, whether you are aware of those beliefs or if they are subconscious drivers.
- Beliefs and values often simmer under the surface, arising as self-awareness increases.
- Instead of gaming the system, get in the game and have some say in the outcome.
- Compromising your beliefs and values may seem to help in the short term, but will limit growth opportunities in the future.

Bringing It All Together

Our beliefs and values not only direct us but make us who we are. From our beliefs and values, our thoughts drive action, or hold us back. Are you attuned to what drives you to think and do the things that you do?

13

Thoughts (and Actions) That Breed Excellence

As we examine, and perhaps modify, our beliefs and values, our thoughts and related actions will follow suit. Managing our thinking game becomes a critical skill as we face adversity, failure, and even success. Our thoughts contain power that can do great good or great damage. As Henry Ford once put it famously, "If you think you can or can't, you're right," which emphasizes how our thoughts determine success or failure.

Many authors have written about positive thinking and how our thoughts can manifest futures or enhance our self-esteem. Psychotherapists will teach us to catch "thinking errors" before they result in unsavory behaviors. With so many resources on the psychology of thinking, I'm going to leave that to the experts. Instead, I'm going to share a few Freedom Frameworks that apply to thought processes, decision-making, communication, and ultimately action.

All Events Are Neutral

All too often, our thoughts get preoccupied with stories we tell ourselves about an event, circumstance, or what others are saying. When we make a judgment about something being right or wrong, good or bad, fair or unfair, we risk allowing our thoughts to get the best of us.

In the movie, *Charlie Wilson's War,* the actor Philip Seymour Hoffman told a story about an old village where a little boy was given a horse. Everyone in the village said, "He's so lucky." Later on in the week, the little boy fell off the horse and broke his leg. Then the villagers said, "That's so sad, he's so unlucky." The very next day, the enemy came to the village and grabbed all the men and children who were able-bodied and took them away as slaves; our lucky/unlucky boy was left behind. You guessed it, the villagers said, "That's great, he is so lucky!"

The moral of the story? The facts are the boy got a horse, fell off the horse, broke his leg, and was left behind. The villagers made up a story at each unveiling of those facts. Was the boy lucky or unlucky? I'd argue neither.

Steve Jobs, who founded Apple once said the best thing that ever happened to him was getting fired by Apple. Some people would get wrapped up in wondering how they could do that. For Jobs, this set into motion a new direction. He started a new company, created a new asset, and would later be hired back. The point (first shared with me by Gabriel Nossovitch, who must have borrowed it from Werner Erhard) is that all experiences are neutral, neither positive nor negative. The only thing positive or negative about experiences is the story we choose to tell ourselves about them.

Things happen to us in life, but it's the story we tell ourselves that makes us feel good or bad about the event. So, if you're going to come up with a story, make sure it's one that works for you positively. Or perhaps even better, avoid making up a story altogether. Just look at the experience as an experience to learn from that can take you one step closer to your goals.

This principle can become one of your greatest allies in life, as well as aid your mental health. We can tie ourselves in knots complaining and holding grudges about bad things that happened to us. These resentments become toxic to relationships, perpetuate fears, and can hold us back from becoming who we want to be. For some reason, the human mind tends to latch onto the negative stories we tell ourselves far longer than any good ones. But there's always two sides to every story. I think the better able we are to stick to the facts, and remain detached from emotional entanglements, the better. Sure, a story may develop from them. But the more we think of experiences as neutral the better.

Some researchers believe we have more than 60,000 thoughts every day. According to the National Science Foundation, 80 percent of our thoughts are negative, and 95 percent of our thoughts are repetitive. Clearly, that's a lot to manage. That's why I started with beliefs and values because they impact our thinking. Combined with these thinking principles, we can make better decisions, keep moving forward, ask better questions, compromise, when possible, relate to others, and protect our psyche along the way.

Master the Questions

The next skill, mastering the questions, is a strategy to assist with our thought process and decision-making. It's the difference between thinking about something, perhaps a decision, feeling the need to feel smart and offer an answer, and asking questions that frame the answer for us. In fact, I believe the key to decision-making is continued curiosity, not necessarily relying on the answers.

Master salespeople are skilled in the art of questions. Through their questions, they can actually get the prospect to answer their own objections. Sales is not only about knowing and believing in your product, it's about helping the prospect to discover why your solution is the answer they've been looking for. Another colleague of mine taught me that "you cannot sell anyone anything; rather you need to focus on helping him buy from you what it is that you want to sell." That's training for another day.

But mastering questions is not for salespeople alone. For example, what is a better question between these two? Where am I going to find a job? Or what specific actions can I take today that may open doors for my next venture? With this simple example, it's easy to see the first question can be answered, "I don't know." While the second question leads the mind into an array of possibilities. And actions.

I mentioned earlier about when I started hosting round tables and created a workflow that systematized the process. While I believe chance favors the prepared, and I prepared vigorously for that first event, the key to improving the system was learning from what we did. After every event, my assistant and I asked ourselves these questions: What went well? What would we do differently? What did we learn? These three questions kept moving us forward, improving our process and outcomes.

Incidentally, hosting a round table requires questions to be developed. I'm continually challenged with identifying the appropriate questions for the panelists and audience. Do I dream them up on my own? Sometimes, but more often, I'm asking the others involved what questions are top of mind for those wanting to be on the panel. I'm asking more questions to identify better questions.

In virtually any setting or circumstance, instead of rushing for data, I'm thinking of better questions to ask. The better the question, the better the data. And with better data, we can make better decisions. Here are a few examples:

Good question: How can we grow our business?

Better question: In what market segment are we sensing an opportunity to increase value for our existing clientele?

Good question: Which job should I take?

Better question: Which job is more fulfilling and will help me grow in my career path?

Good question: Where should we go to lunch?

Better question: What sounds better for lunch: Mexican, Italian, or sandwiches?

As you can probably see in these examples, mastering the art of asking questions will be a skill that will help you in more ways than one. Last, let me make a distinction with a difference. Asking a better question is better than asking a question. But asking more questions is better than both. The mastery is in continuing to ask questions rather than alternatively being quick to find a solution.

The Shark Theory

Too often, we can think (or indeed question) ourselves into the tar pit. We believe we can *think* our way to the top. But, I believe, another key to success is to *do* our way to the top. Thinking can only get you to process more data. But when you do something, you are moving forward and gaining experience and intelligence in the process. You are acquiring skills, accumulating experiences, and developing relationships. To me, I'd rather jump in the pool and start swimming to find answers, than stay on the deck thinking about what to do next.

This is the basis for what I call the shark theory. I'm not referring to "swimming with sharks," as in dealing with ruthless people. Instead, I'm talking about a mindset for making progress and decisions.

First, we have to understand a bit about the shark: Most fish have swim bladders, which are pockets of air that keep them from sinking. But not the shark. Moreover, the shark body can be compared to an airplane wing to help provide lift. Since sharks only have one asymmetrical tail fin on their back, it appears they are created to move forward at all times, or they will sink.

Therefore, regardless of the circumstance, relationship, or challenge at play, I like to apply the shark theory and keep swimming forward.

Often, we can get stuck in our tracks with paralysis by analysis. Of course, we need to think through decisions, but overthinking can be a downfall as well. No decision is still a decision. At some point, we must decide what's best for the platform, and for our career, based on the data, our experience, and perhaps our gut feelings. Still, when you simply don't know what to do, sometimes the best decision is to not make a decision while still moving forward.

How do you put a decision on hold while moving forward?

I refer to asking more questions and using the three keys to success: acquire skills, accumulate experiences, and develop relationships. Then, honoring our beliefs and values, we can keep exploring, even when we're not 100 percent sure about what's next. Remember, there is a difference between taking on a future problem prematurely and doing whatever you can today to avoid a problem in the future. Sometimes not making a decision is prudent. Just keep moving forward until it is time to decide and take new action.

To clarify, the shark theory is not a decision-making principle. It's a thinking and doing principle. It's about moving forward with small steps toward a goal. Sharks don't always know exactly where they are going to find their next meal, so they keep moving forward or else they sink.

If you really don't know what to do, then don't make the decision. I don't mean standing around and doing nothing. Instead, keep exploring, keep asking questions, and sharpen your saw, as Stephen Covey put it. At some point, you will reach a tipping point. However, when you know what to do, and you allow the fear of making a mistake to put your progress on hold, that's when you're overplaying the whole thing.

When people look for answers to solve a problem, they think a decision must be made. But some decisions can wait, while we search for data that better help us answer the problem. That is moving forward, and perhaps moving forward even more wisely. Sometimes, people make a decision and then find data to support the decision. I fall into this when I am trying to be more comfortable with a decision. That could be called confirmation bias; however, that's moving forward as well. The point is to avoid paralysis by analysis by applying the shark theory.

Quick Takes

- The more neutral we see our own experiences, the less we become defined by them. Or at least thrown by them.
- Let's make sure our stories aren't subconsciously about proving ourselves right about our belief system .
- Be curious and master the art of asking better questions.
- Use the shark theory to avoid paralysis by analysis.

Bringing It All Together

I suggest we work from a foundation of beliefs and values that drive our thoughts, and that's why this chapter is about tools in our utility belt for driving more productive action. As we believe that all events are neutral, that the only thing positive or negative about an event is the stories we tell ourselves about the event, we learned how we, and others, process our actions. The shark theory keeps us moving forward, and we remember to ask more, and better, questions.

14

Joy on the Journey—Be Yourself

Success can be a self-fulfilling prophecy. On the journey, we grab our destiny by accumulating gumballs with every new skill, new experience, and relationship. We've envisioned an intended future, assessed our current reality, and executed a transition plan. Yet, success is not the destination. Success is a reward, or outcome, of source activities.

I think true joy and fulfillment comes from the journey of the growth process and it is never ending. Happiness is peripatetic, and if we get caught chasing that, our destination will look much different from what we intended.

Along the way, we expect mistakes, obstacles, and even roadblocks to test our resolve, mindset, and skill sets. That's when we need to exercise a fundamental framework to propel us forward while preserving our joy on the journey and the success of our self-fulfilling prophecy.

Bad judgment leads to bad experiences; however, bad experiences ultimately lead to good judgment, which leads to good experiences.

Experience and Judgment

This profoundly simple idea helps us to learn from our mistakes, instead of wallowing in them. Essentially, I'm encouraging poor judgment (and to "do" rather than to wait and to "think" or overthink to keep moving, as in The Shark Theory introduced in the previous chapter) because I know it should lead, eventually, to good judgment. There's no such thing as a good judgment pill that we can swallow. So how do we learn good judgment? From bad experiences resulting from bad judgment.

How many times did you think you were doing the right thing? Always, right? And only through a bad experience did you realize, whoops, that was a bad decision. I'm okay with bad decisions because they lead us to higher ground. The only competitive advantage we as humans have is how fast we recognize a mistake and course correct with a new action caused by how much and how fast we have learned from an experience. It follows my principle that prefers overdoing rather than overthinking. Through doing, we gain experiences. So, the iconoclast executive makes allowances for mistakes because they are only lessons learned.

Well, then how do we know if we made a mistake? There was a bad experience we didn't enjoy, or we didn't like the outcome of our source activity. What drove the bad experience? A bad decision. Why did you make a bad decision? Poor judgment. Now, we arrive at the root of the issue/opportunity. What did we learn from that poor judgment? If we make a better decision next time, it leads to a good experience.

Plus, later on, when looking back at the bad experience, we can get a good chuckle about it.

Avoid the Joy Killer

While pursuing career independence, avoid what I call the joy killer. It's the trap we set for ourselves when comparing ourselves with others. Wyatt fell into that trap (with his siblings), and it affected his belief in himself. But once he pulled himself out of that trap, his own journey began to be illuminated. If we allow envy or jealousy to motivate us, then we'll swing from vine to vine trying to find someone else's happiness, which is a temporary emotion that needs more fuel.

When we compare ourselves to others, there will always be something missing that we want. I don't care if you're a multi-millionaire, you'll want what the billionaire has. Instead, joy can be found in the journey of making progress. The only person to compare yourself with is you. You are your greatest asset, and you can control what you think about, what you do, and how you do it. Focus on your dreams, aspirations, and intended future; compare your progress to that. Not to a peer or random person.

So instead of focusing on what we don't have, let's focus on what we do have. And if you want a different outcome, the only thing that matters is to focus on the source activities that get you there.

The Loss of Perspective

Imagine you're at one edge of Lake Michigan. Your goal is to swim across. You've trained for this moment and believed you have the strength and endurance to accomplish this 118-mile swim. It's just you, the lake, and your belief. So, you start swimming. Periodically, you look back to see how far you've come, which energizes you with joy and fulfillment. But then, you get to the midway mark, and you no longer can see where you've been and you're not far enough to see where you want to be.

Suddenly, a demon pops up in the form of dread, fear, and doubt.

In that moment, your belief that you have what it takes gets questioned. What was I thinking? The water is so cold. Why didn't I wear a wet suit? You ask yourself. You may even think about raising the white flag of surrender and hailing a boat for help. Life and death seem to be on the line.

But something inside tells you to push through the fear and keep swimming. Keep your eyes on the prize, you tell yourself, even though you can't see the goal.

So, you swim and swim some more. Pretty soon, you look up and you can see the other shore. Motivation kicks in. I can do this, you think, and replace the demon with hope. Now, no matter how tired you are, your belief in accomplishing the task strengthens. At one time, looking back motivated you. Now, looking ahead builds upon the motivation that was temporarily paused.

The moral of the story is that every hard project will place us right in the middle of Lake Michigan. We will inevitably get to the spot where we are disoriented, where we can't remember how far we've come, and we have no idea where we are going or why. That's when we need to exercise discipline, persistence, and grit, and have faith in ourselves or something else to help us keep pushing through when there's no end in sight, or when we lose sight of how far we have come.

The old joke is when you are going through hell, just keep on going! We have to keep our eyes on the prize, and in our case, the prize is our self-proclaimed intended future.

Our human impulses are interesting. Although they are often rooted in our beliefs, impulses can also lead us astray. The swimmer in the middle of Lake Michigan had a natural impulse to quit, despite proper training and preparation. For a moment, he lost belief in himself and forgot about all his training. However, he decided to keep swimming because discipline kicked in, overpowering his own moment of mental weakness.

When you think about it, the most powerful superpower any of us possess is our own willpower.

The tough love is this: Achieving your intended future, or economic independence, will require discipline, persistence, and time. This is where grit and perseverance matter. There will be moments when you feel as if you're in the middle of Lake Michigan, ready to give up. But that's exactly when to exercise discipline and the shark theory to keep swimming forward, one stroke at a time. Believe in yourself. Remind yourself why you're heading in that direction and turn those demons into catalysts. Along the way, you will experience the reward of self-satisfaction that you never gave up while achieving a massive goal.

This is where grit and persistence matter. Psychologist Angela Duckworth wrote a book called *Grit*. She has done extensive research on what determines success. She studied thousands of individuals at the US Military Academy at West Point and at the National Spelling Bee as well as salespeople and rookie teachers in tough neighborhoods.

The answer she writes about is not IQ, wealth, race, or physical prowess. The answer she proclaims is grit, which she defined as "passion and perseverance for very long-term goals." It's the ability to stick with a difficult task, not for weeks or months but for years. Grit, she teaches us "empowers us to live life like it's a marathon not a sprint."

There have been times in my journey where I found myself stuck in the middle of Lake Michigan where I could see neither the Chicago skyline or the Michigan shore. They included my initial college application rejection to Stanford, my work for the Kellogg Corporation, and my early years at Cohen Financial. The family business conflicts with first my father and then my brother Bruce. My fight for justice over Darren Shirlaw, the failed expansion and market-induced regression of Cohen Financial. Fighting through the cycles of the real estate economy.

In hindsight, I don't know how I ever got through them all. But in each case, with perseverance I found sight of the Michigan shore and completed another part of the journey. You can and will do it too.

You may not be where you want to be, and when you look back, you can't see how far you've come. But the fact is, you have come a long way, and you can reach your goal. You're just in a position where you need to have faith in the process and keep on keeping on. Besides, I know this for a fact —

Life is hard if you only do the easy things, and easy if you do the hard things.

Eccentric and Weird

One day when I was twenty-four and working for my dad,

my dad came over to my desk and asked "Jack, are you busy?"

"Uh, no, Dad. I'm eating chocolate bonbons and waiting to have my nails done. What do you mean? Am I busy? Of course, I'm busy," I said.

"Grab your coat," he demanded.

"Where are we going? Can't it wait?"

"We're going to see Sam Zell," he said.

"Who?"

I didn't realize my dad was taking me to meet the most iconoclast commercial real estate investor and ultimate rogue executive I'd ever meet and who would share something that has stuck with me for the last forty-three years.

On the way, my dad told me that when Sam was at the University of Michigan as a college student, he started buying student housing, and my dad banked him. Over the years, they built a mutually beneficial relationship, part mentor/mentee, part collaborator. Sam had lived in the town I grew up in, Highland Park, Illinois. And the temple that I went to had the main sanctuary named the Zell Sanctuary.

My dad would sponsor the building of a religious school and name it after my grandparents, the Jack and Mildred Cohen Religious School. My dad was so proud of having a building named after his parents where the Jewish religious school education would continue. At least until he found out that the way Sam contributed his capital was through an instrument called a zero-coupon bond.

In a moment of weakness, my dad was joyless that Sam had created a better vehicle for accomplishing the same thing my dad had done, and that got under his skin. Remember, comparison is the enemy of joy. But that's not the point of the story.

We went to an office building where my dad had partial ownership, and where Sam leased office space. We went up the elevator. When the door opened, this man and my dad started trading barbs, shouting at one another like a verbal boxing match. Sam led us to his office, and I was mortified. I had never seen anyone interact with my dad like that before. I pulled my chair out of the line of fire hoping Sam wouldn't notice me.

That didn't work.

Mid-tirade, Sam turned to me and said, "Young man." I looked away hoping he wasn't addressing me. "I'm talking to you."

"Yes, Mr. Zell," I finally replied.

"Do you know the difference between eccentric and weird?"

"No, sir."

Without missing a beat, Sam said, "Talent."

Sam passed away May 18, 2023, as an eighty-one-year-old multibillionaire. While he ventured into several businesses, his primary laboratory was the commercial real estate industry as founder of Equity Group Investments and Equity Office, which he sold to Blackstone for $39 billion. He fashioned himself as a grave dancer, with a nose for scooping up underperforming assets at low costs and turning them into profitable assets.

As savvy as he was, Sam was also as irreverent as they ever came. The things I'd never say on a phone call, he'd say from the stage. His brand was provocative, and he behaved as counter cultural as anyone.

Ben Johnson wrote *Money Talks, Bullsh*t Walks: Inside the Contrarian Mind of Billionaire Sam Zell*, based on interviews and research about Sam. But I knew I had one very real Sam experience, and even aspired to be like him. If Sam wasn't successful, everyone would've thought he was weird. But he had talent, so that made him eccentric, and he owned it. He made it his brand, and he never shied away from being himself.

Sam was also self-sufficient and knew success was a self-fulfilling prophecy. If he didn't know something, he learned it. If he didn't know somebody, he found a way to meet that person. Along the way, he accumulated experiences that gave him knowledge that he converted into intelligence. But it was how he approached life that became his calling card. Even if Sam did not become one of the most successful investors ever, his life would leave a lasting impression on everyone he met.

This whole book is about trusting and having faith in yourself and taking these tools to reach further so you have freedom to choose what's best for you. The implication is that you can stray outside the norm for a worthy cause. Society honors living conformists (and, yet somehow, the dead non-conformists). But the outliers, the self-sufficient, nonconformist executives are seemingly way behind or way out in front of the curve. They may seem weird or eccentric, but they may have hidden talents yet to be revealed in the journey. And for some reason, they will be the ones remembered after they are gone. So, it's okay to be rogue and think differently. Own it, and it will take you places you always thought were possible.

Quick Takes

- Mistakes are lessons in disguise. Bad judgment leads to bad experiences, but bad experiences lead to good judgment, which leads to good experiences.

- Don't fall for the joy killer. Focus on what you have, not on what's missing.
- Choose to enjoy the journey of making progress toward your goals.
- Have faith in yourself when you have lost sight of where you came from, can't see the shores of your destination, and feel dead in the water.
- Adopt a self-sufficient mindset to achieve your self-fulfilling prophecy.

Bringing It All Together

Life is hard if you only do the easy stuff, and easy if you do the hard stuff. Happiness might be peripatetic. Comparison is the enemy of joy. As you acquire skills, accumulate experiences, and develop relationships, you will become more talented. Talent converts people's view of you from weird to eccentric. Own who you are. Be.

15

Honest Confessions

"Hi, I'm Jack, and I'm a . . . workaholic," at least that's what my wife thinks. I'd rather say that I am a striver who has an insatiable appetite for various forms of success. Either way, this approach to life, career, and relationships can be problematic. That's why I want to make some honest confessions with you in the next few pages, because taking an inventory of your assets and liabilities—with regard to your character and temperament—will help you avoid going into (and through) your career wearing blinders.

We need to recognize our strengths and weaknesses, learning how to leverage our assets and minimize potential for collateral damage from our liabilities. There's nothing more emotionally intelligent than having the self-awareness that you may be the problem and being able to course correct quickly.

I have a successful colleague who admits to being a high-maintenance, impossible HR problem. He'd say his management style is this: "I got dumped on early in my career and look how I turned out. So, I'm gonna dump on you." To me, even though I was dumped on, I felt it was unnecessary, so I never want to do that to others. Rather, I have always wanted to pave the way and make it easier for the next generation.

I once asked him, "I don't understand, every one of your friends outside of work are the nicest people I have ever met in my life. How do they put up with you?"

He said, "Jack, I am such an ass. The only people who are willing to stay with me have to be really nice human beings."

At least he was self-aware and honest about it. Now let me be honest with you.

I begin with my assets.

I am an overachiever and overpreparer possibly because I had a second-guessing micromanaging father. I have always been thorough. I'm a top performer, not because I'm talented, but because I work hard. I have energy. I am a lifelong learner. I cross-train and have made a varied, maybe unconventional, successful career out of acquiring skills, accumulating experiences, and developing relationships. I strive to improve. I connect the dots pretty well, which allows me to apply something today that I learned last month.

I may tick somebody off with radical candor, but I recognize (more and more) quickly when I say something hurtful. I've always been fast to apologize, but I am not always as quick to understand that I created collateral damage. I may say something that lands with another as disrespectful, but I'll own it and course correct faster and faster as I get better and better at recognizing it.

As much as my career has been defined by relationships, collaboration, and learning from mentors, I have demons that indeed include character liabilities. I am told I can be intimidating and intense. Even if the circumstance calls for radical candor, my own temperament and tone can drive people away. I get impatient with dumb decision-making processes. Do I suffer fools poorly? Yeah. Do I come across arrogant or condescending? Probably (though not intentionally).

I'm mindful of the fact that a lot of people hear my words as judgmental. Do people see me as soft and cuddly? Probably not. But of all my liabilities, the one I personally struggle with the most is controlling my anger. And nobody wants to work with a radically candid grump who is hostile.

I don't pretend to be a know-it-all or perfect by any stretch of the imagination. But I do aspire to a high standard of excellence which drives me to expect others to do so as well. When my standards aren't met, through my own efforts or by another, I get frustrated with my own choices or with others' apparent incompetence. Maybe that's why I have always liked the late, great Bobby Knight, the basketball coach who was famous for losing his cool. He also had a very successful coaching career, winning 902 games over forty-two seasons at Army, Indiana, and Texas Tech, losing only 371 games for a remarkable .709 winning percentage.

How did I end up like the Bobby Knight of commercial real estate finance?

I'm a product of my conditioning (much like many of us). I've spent decades living and working in close quarters with some of the angriest people I've ever known. One was my dad. He was a pent-up menace who loved to fight. He was a nice and charming man. Largely, he was respectful and gracious to others. But boy did he have a temper and a short fuse. He got into many fistfights as a child and through his college years. When he got older, they turned into personal conflicts with other business professionals. To his dying day, there were people he was still mad at. So, when I grew up, I didn't know any other way. I always had an angry father, and I thought it was normal to welcome anger into my daily life.

Maybe my dad had a right to be angry. He was twenty-five when his father passed away of a heart attack. He was his hero. His idol. His best friend. No matter, it's not for me to justify or for me to play the victim card on his behalf. Though a screamer, my dad loved me and my siblings, and he never ever raised a hand to us. By no means was I abused.

Still, anger can cloud judgment. I constantly have to work on lengthening my fuse and not blowing my top. It doesn't help that what comes out of my mouth can be hurtful, and it's embarrassing to clean up. But mostly, it fosters bad judgment and decision-making (not to mention behavior).

Some liabilities come from conditioning and genetics. I'm not suggesting you need to ruminate over why you have a certain liability. However, it can help in understanding yourself. Still, that doesn't excuse those liabilities. The sooner we can acknowledge the chinks in our armor, the sooner we can do something about it. For me, I must exercise vigorously to quiet the storm that can erupt at inopportune times.

Radical Candor

Kim Scott wrote a wonderful book called *Radical Candor®*. Again, oversimplifying this concept (much like I did with Market Force, OKRs, *Grit*, and time management), she draws a correlation between how much you care about people and how direct you are in your communications. On a vertical axis we plot how much we care about people (the top is Care, the bottom is Don't care); on the horizontal axis we plot how direct we are in our interaction with people (on left is Indirect, on right is Direct). This creates four quadrants.

Radical Candor

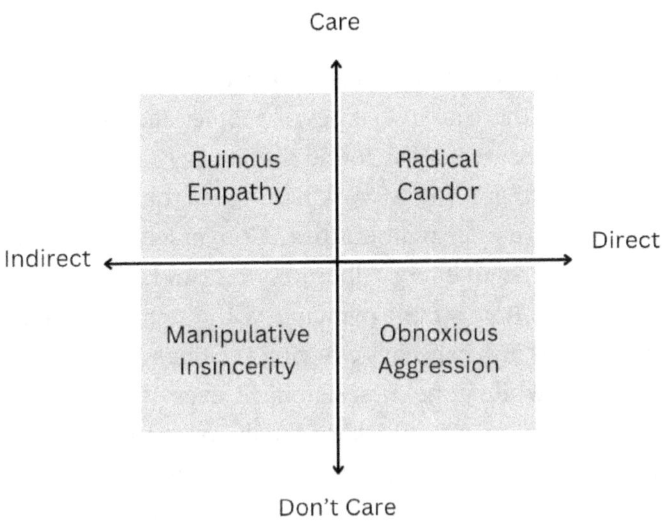

Figure 19   Source: Kim Scott

Where do you stand on a scale of care about people vs comfort with direct communication?

I care very deeply about helping people. I like people. I live in a world of direct communications (maybe too direct?). This is where Kim Scott suggests that I live in a world of radical candor. By comparison, one of my CEO colleagues is as much a caring relationship professional as I am (maybe more). However, he abhors direct conversations that are hard for him to have. Kim Scott refers to this as unintentional but ruinous empathy. Yes, it's bad, not helpful.

Note: I am ignoring the two quadrants below the caring line because why would you want to interact with someone who doesn't like people and is overly direct (obnoxious) or overly indirect (manipulative)?

Energy Liberators and Energy Consumers

I've learned there are two types of people: energy liberators and energy consumers. I've found that energy consumers tend to trigger my anger. I now work hard to surround myself, the best I can, with energy liberators. Conversely, I've learned that I need to be an energy liberator so I can facilitate better collaboration. It's a simple principle with massive rewards.

Throughout my early days working at Cohen Financial with my dad, and while in my first marriage, everywhere I turned, energy consumers were sucking the life out of me. I became an angry, ambitious man who needed a new platform that was more conducive to my career and relational growth.

Perhaps this personal awareness will help you pick the right platform with people and a culture that lift your growth opportunities and limit exposure to your liabilities.

Applying what you know about your character balance sheet made of assets and liabilities is really where the rubber meets the road. For example, recently I spoke with a client, the CEO of a major finance company, about why the platform doesn't get things done, among other items. My honest, unfiltered explanation was, "I believe the culture here does not support radical candor. As such, the platform is political and gossipy. The end result is there's this kind of backroom culture that doesn't talk about our issues head on. Instead, they percolate and get dealt off to the side, which hinders progress on real issues."

Immediately, the CEO appeared to get defensive, asking me, "Do you think I'm the problem?"

"Well, we all hold this responsibility. But let me explain this another way. For example, I often think out loud. My mind consolidates information as I speak. You, on the other hand, think while others are talking. We're at two ends of the spectrum. While I believe the best idea wins, I'm open and transparent, and I like dialogue, I'm also mindful of the fact that I am intense, which is intimidating for people. Do people really say their truth in my presence? Not always. That's on me. That's not the organization's responsibility."

I continued, "On the flip side, you are an excellent relationship guy. You learn when people are venting, essentially listening to gossip to get information on the organization. Both you and I, collectively and unintentionally, produce an unproductive, unsafe environment for people to talk about what they're afraid of or what motivates them or where the problems are."

I share this example because both this CEO and I had to recognize our liabilities and make adjustments in order to create a culture that has the capability of facing problems, instead of sidestepping them.

* * *

I can't really tell you why, but this anger of mine has been raising its ugly head recently. Maybe it's a slope growth issue or feeling like I'm spinning my wheels. I'm not kicking dogs and screaming at my wife, but I can see how anger tends to cloud my judgment. Although I know humans are human and

I try not to imbue others' intent, I feel a little off the rails. It was perfect timing for Yom Kippur this year.

Every Yom Kippur (or Day of Atonement, a Jewish holiday celebrating repentance and forgiveness of sins), I go to temple to think about my sins and pray to be inscribed in the Book of Life. I always think about what I really want, and that's peace of mind. I reflect on the year that went by and wonder if I've made progress or not. I'm a work in progress too. The musician, John Mayer, has a song on his Continuum album called "In Repair" with lyrics that say, "I'm in repair…I am not together but I am getting there." My oldest son gravitates to this message, even getting a tattoo on his arm that says, "In repair."

Therefore, I reach my final confession: I, too, am in repair.

Now, let's turn the tables. How about you?

In a notebook or journal, take some time to honestly inventory your own behavioral balance sheet, listing your assets and liabilities.

Here are a few questions to help the process:

- What kind of market force participant do you think you are? (Refer to chapter 9 regarding control, power, influence, and authority.) Why do you think that?
- What assets do you bring to the table? (Think strengths.)
- What interaction liabilities seem to pop up frequently? (Think weaknesses.)
- What assets can you leverage better?
- What liabilities can you improve upon and minimize?
- What's the behavioral bottom line? For example, I'm a driven striver who employs influence to get ahead. However, I can turn people away with my candid, off-

putting remarks. If I can be more compassionate with others, I can improve the dynamics of my team.

Quick Takes

- Leverage your character and temperament assets. Minimize potential for collateral damage from your liabilities.
- Surround yourself with energy liberators. Avoid energy consumers.
- Live in a world of radical candor (respectfully, of course).
- Ultimate success comes with a mindset that we are all in repair.

Bringing It All Together

Anger gets in my way. It clouds my judgment, and it gets in the way of my using the tools in my utility belt. What character flaws might you have that contribute to holding you back from achieving success on your own terms?

16

Where Do You Go from Here?

Like Bruce Wayne's struggle to balance his career leading Wayne Enterprises with his passion for fighting crime, we will all have "what if" questions, like "What if I just let someone else run Wayne Enterprises?" In our reality, we will all have to answer a question like this: "When is it time to move on from this path?"

That's where I find myself, as I write these words.

I began the book by revealing that I feared not having a dream. Fast-forward and I'm realizing my dream(s) but now I'm caught in the all-too-familiar quandary of "Should I stay or should I go."

Earlier in the book, I mentioned that I have been working at ArrowMark Partners, which employs lovely people who are respectful, honorable, and patient with my idiosyncratic tendencies. They have been a great audience for my stories and frameworks. They also have been exceptional students, willingly learning what I had to teach and share. But the itch started surfacing right about the time I started writing this book.

I believe there is nothing more I can do, no more to share, no more to teach to help the ArrowMark commercial real estate team operate a business better, faster, and more effectively. Yet, I'm filled with uncertainty, because a part of me wants to be a part of helping this organization continue to reach new heights.

What motivates me, what drives me, what gets me out of bed in the morning to go to work is helping a team operate their business better. I want to keep helping leadership teams, help them build world-class businesses like I hope I have done with Cohen Financial, Shirlaws, 3650 REIT, Stronghill Capital, and ArrowMark.

My standard of excellence, which defines right and wrong, tells me I can't really look for the next gig while I am currently working at ArrowMark. I know folks tell you that it's easiest to look for a job while you are employed (let alone have the continuation of compensation), yet it doesn't feel right to me.

Resistance, uncertainty, doubt, self-flagellation crept in. What to do? I have an internal battle between what drives me and my intended future against a demon that's putting me into a holding pattern.

The folks at ArrowMark have been simply wonderful to me. When I asked to reduce my compensation so I could work less during the summer, they never hesitated. They have always been supportive of my articulated needs. Further, I genuinely love, respect, and admire them all. How can I leave? There is unfinished business here at the platform, and I should want to be part of that journey, right?

Still, I have felt the urge to help another business grow. Something inside me wants to find a business that could benefit from my experiences with operating businesses. I find myself telling myself negative stories that aren't helpful. My system is searching for a justification, looking to manufacture evidence that it's time to let go of the vine.

I began my swing to another vine recently when Arrow-Mark announced it was time to renew enrollment for health insurance. I told my boss that I was feeling my job was done, that I was feeling an itch to find another business to help. I asked if we could convert my employment status to consultant (my Darkknight Ventures business) and hang around for a few specific tasks on a consulting arrangement. Of course, he offered support but wanted me to know that there is unfinished business at ArrowMark, and he personally wanted me to stay. What a guy. What a boss, What a friend.

What should I do? Leave? Stay? Something in between?

At the same time, a friend of mine in Aspen, Colorado, is building an extremely successful alternative asset manager in the residential space. He does not need me to help him envision, create, or grow this business or to make money. To his credit, he realized that none of the members of his thirty-nine-plus and growing-person professional team had operating experience. They have grown fast, built three solid legs to the stool of their business, and made more than a dozen investments in other businesses that made up the ecosystem surrounding his business, Saluda Grade.

Would I have time to help him institutionalize his business? Would I have an interest in helping connect the individual parts of the ecosystem to create some sort of connection that synergistically turbocharges the entire ecosystem? Could I act as a mentor to him and his team and additionally act as head of strategy for the entire platform of operating units?

Wow! Sounds great. Right?

What is holding me back? Hello demon named resistance.

I know the commercial real estate (CRE) space. My rolodex means something in the commercial capital markets. I've excelled in this space and respect everyone at ArrowMark. However, I am not the Bobby Knight of residential real estate. Maybe I should play it safe and stay the course.

As this wheel of indecision comes around, I admit to not feeling nourished. I have said that I feel my purpose is to learn and experience, so I can teach and help others optimize their journey. While I have participated in the CRE capital markets for more than forty-three years, I always felt I was an operator. Strategic. An industry spokesperson.

Saluda Grade would offer me a mentoring, coaching, operating opportunity. But it's in a space I do not know—residential. But four years ago, when presented with the opportunity to help Stronghill Capital, I remembered the doubt I had about that opportunity because its space, small balance commercial, was a space I did not know. That worked out; maybe this might too.

I am swinging on that vine of routine. My current reality is safe. Pleasant. Comfortable. I can do as much or as little as I choose. It plays to my strength. I have invested a lot of money with the team at ArrowMark and in their first fund. Yet, I am releasing the grip on one of my hands and looking for another vine to reach for.

My purpose is to make my experiences available to others to help them optimize their journey. My gift is to give that away. Saluda Grade is asking for my help, to join their team.

I'm in a place where I have to practice what I preach. What frameworks and principles should I apply from this book?

When I last did my current reality to intended future

planning, I looked out thirty years—when I would be ninety-three. I am active. I enjoy my wife, children, and grandchildren. I had monthly cash flow to support my lifestyle.

I never wanted a business that I run to be about my lifestyle. As an entrepreneur, I always wanted to be institutional and build a business that creates wealth for others so that business could outlive the current leadership team. The founder and CEO of Saluda Grade is that kind of CEO. He is building wealth in his business and in other businesses and is asking for my help. Saluda Grade is not a lifestyle business; he is trying to institutionalize it, so it outlives him.

Although I am happy now, my work isn't joyful. I am scared, but I am reaching for a new challenge. I am certainly not running from anything; I am running to another place where I can help others optimize their journey and build a world-class business.

But what if I fail? What if my failure creates collateral damage in my relationship with my friend? What if I miss something great happening at ArrowMark?

Resistance. Sleepless nights. My subconscious is trying to protect me. I've never been more on the fence about anything.

If I think about the shark theory, I'd move forward and grab the next vine. I mentioned earlier in the book that money is not typically the real issue when leaving a job. It's more about the environment. That's partly true in my case. For example, in the last few months, I've recognized I am no longer the master of my own calendar. I have to slow down and wait for others or the organization to make decisions. That's fine, but it's affecting my own cadence. I feel like a thoroughbred caught in a cage.

This cadence issue has dusted off the Curious George inside

me. I have a bit of a wandering eye. Perhaps, I've finished my work here and am curious about the opportunity at Saluda Grade. If I think through the long game principle, then I could envision always being available for ArrowMark because of the mutual respect we've built. Perhaps the answer is to create a win-win-win for all parties? But what would that look like?

If I swoop over to Saluda Grade, the speed of execution entices me. Residential real estate continues to have high demand. Plus, I'll cross-train learning new skills, accumulate new experiences, and develop new relationships. It would be safe to stick around with ArrowMark, but at what opportunity cost? One point in favor of Saluda Grade is that they have an office in New York City, where I could visit my childrens' families more often.

Despite the uncertainties around such a move, I decided to negotiate a consulting arrangement with ArrowMark, while taking on a new role with Saluda Grade to create a win-win-win. I went for the new vine. Before I even started, I felt passion renewing, energy boosting, and focus unleashing. Still, I also feel like I'm swimming in the middle of Lake Michigan, and my demons are pouncing.

In my work with Saluda Grade, I am the only professional with experience in the commercial real estate space. At the time of this writing, I am trying to figure out how to bring small balance commercial loan securitization to Saluda Grade and eventually expand Saluda Grade offerings to include income-producing finance of the multifamily asset class. Honestly, I don't know enough yet to make this happen.

I have originated small and large balance CRE loans; I have never securitized them. I don't know how the bonds are priced. I think I know what a good loan looks like, but I have never built out a program from scratch. Using the shark theory I keep asking questions, talking to colleagues, enhancing my education on the topic, reading what others have done, as I am still trying to grasp the lay of the land at Saluda Grade, an alternate asset manager in the residential space.

I don't know if this will work out, but in the end, I'm going to keep swimming, reaching out to grab my career destiny with the tools I've acquired.

That's what I hope for you.

Mantra for the Iconoclast Executive

*Society honors living conformists
and dead non-conformists.*

The Freedom Frameworks at a Glance

(In alphabetical order)

Acknowledgments

They say it takes a village to raise a child. Well, I think it also pertains to our professional careers as well. Forgive me in advance if I somehow forgot to specifically name you. Please know that I have taken wisdom from every professional exchange and grown. Every ship that has passed mine in the night somehow made a difference in the man you now see before you.

I want to thank David Jahr, my stunt double. You stood by my side coaching, teaching, interviewing, and even writing with, and for, me to make this book a reality. I want to thank Donna Galassi for helping me find David. I want to thank Jared Cohen for introducing me to Donna.

I thank my wife and children; they are the students who truly became my teachers.

I thank Dr. Aleen Bayard, Gabrial Nossovitch, Delynn Copley, Debbie McAneny, Sam Davis, Tom Wilson, Curtis Mass, Steve Perlman, Rick Woldenberg, Jordan Dorfman, John Petrovski, Gadi Kaufman, Matt Levy, Stew Gall, Darren Shirlaw, Lee Cotton, Cody Smith, Bruce Cohen, Cory Olson, Coach Hansen, Mr. Suber, Dr. Jack Merrick, Jared Cohen, Jack Taylor, Sam Saxton, Bill Shoptaw, Bob Foley, Bob Dzuibla, Stan Nevin, and General John L. Putnam of the USAF for all the lessons you have taught me in our daily interactions, sparring, and one-on-one dinners.

I am blessed to have had good academic teachers and admirable managers and coworkers.

Last, I want to specially acknowledge the support given to me by Nancy Cohen and Diane Valha. Each of them individually are my very own "Jane/Alfred/Q/Gandhi/Ma cGyver" all in one. I simply can't be me without them.

With respect, love, admiration, and appreciation for all, thank you.

LET'S KEEP THE
CONVERSATION GOING

Book Jack Cohen for speaking engagements at **darkknightventures.net/keynote-speaker**.

Join Jack's email list to receive exclusive content. Visit **darkknightventures.net/the-freedom-frameworks** to sign up.

CONNECT WITH JACK AT...

LinkedIn: Jack M. Cohen

About the Author

Jack M. Cohen describes himself as an iconoclast executive and a mentor capitalist who invests intellectual and economic capital to help individuals and corporations accelerate growth. A respected management and finance professional with more than forty-three years' experience in commercial real estate, Jack worked at, and eventually led, Cohen Financial for thirty-five years, participating in a team of exceptional executives who grew the platform from producing $200 million of origination and servicing to a high–water mark of $6 billion in origination and $35 billion in servicing. He also participated in the recapitalization of the firm six times between 1998 and 2013.

He earned a Bachelor of Arts from Claremont Men's College (today known as Claremont McKenna College) and a bachelor of science in civil engineering and a master's degree in construction management from Stanford University.

Jack founded Darkknight Ventures, LLC to lend guidance to C-suite leadership, entrepreneurs, and young professionals seeking to develop superior skills, advance careers, create and manage high-performance teams, grow revenue, arrange capital formation, and facilitate corporate recapitalization, scaling, and organization strategy.

Jack's diverse portfolio of career initiatives includes current and previous roles as a non-executive vice-chairman at 3650 REIT, a board member and investor at CRESimple, Hillcrest, B+E, Ascot, Forum Real Estate Group, and Academic Approach. He currently advises ArrowMark Partners, a $24 billion investment management firm, while serving as head of strategy at Saluda Grade, a multibillion-dollar residential real estate asset management and investment firm.

His contributions to the industry have been recognized with several honors and awards including the CREFC (Commercial Real Estate Finance Council) Founder's Award in recognition of lifetime contributions to the commercial real estate securitization industry.

With a passion to serve, Jack has several professional affiliations, including association president of Chartered Realty Investor and Commercial Real Estate Finance Council, Commercial Real Estate Finance/Multifamily Board of Governors, and the big board at the Mortgage Bankers Association. Additionally, Jack is active with the Young Presidents' Organization. He's also a popular round table host, forum moderator, and guest speaker.

Personally, Jack maintains an Airline Transport Pilot license and two Single Pilot type ratings for flying light jets. A fan of the iconoclast Batman and James Bond characters, Jack is also a second-degree black belt in Tomiki-style Aikido, a NAUI-certified scuba diver, an active CrossFitter, and loves rock climbing.

He is based in Aspen, Colorado, where he lives with his wife, Nancy. Jack has three sons and a daughter: Wyatt, Alec (married to Niki), and Jared (married to Rachel) along with Lindsay (married to Brandon). Jack also has three new grandchildren (Jude Morrison Cohen, Brylee Grace Richter, and Bella Clare Abrams).

You can connect with me on:
- http://www.darkknightventures.net
- https://www.linkedin.com/in/jack-m-cohen-9543269